Transition in Africa:
Studies in Political Adaptation

THE AFRICAN RESEARCH SERIES

With TRANSITION IN AFRICA, *the African Research and Studies Program of Boston University introduces a new occasional series,* AFRICAN RESEARCH STUDIES. *The Program was founded in 1953 as one manifestation of the increasing involvement of American scholarship in the field of African studies. The number of scholars now writing on African matters is increasing rapidly and the desirability of a publication medium devoted exclusively to the African area is obvious.* AFRICAN RESEARCH STUDIES *will have a dual purpose: to present informed discussions of current trends in Africa; and to contribute to basic research in the disciplines of the social sciences which are today drawing an increasing body of data from research in Africa. The series will provide a medium for the appearance of discussions which fall between the full-length book and the short article normally published in the professional journals; these may be the work of a single author or a symposium by a number of different scholars concerned with a single theme. A standard format will be maintained throughout the series, but hard or soft covers will be used depending upon the length of the contribution. It is hoped that the new series will prove a useful medium to all those scholars interested in the development of African studies.*

WILLIAM O. BROWN, Director
African Research and Studies Program

Transition in Africa:

STUDIES IN POLITICAL ADAPTATION

GWENDOLEN M. CARTER AND WILLIAM O. BROWN, Editors

AFRICAN RESEARCH STUDIES NO. 1

AFRICAN RESEARCH AND STUDIES PROGRAM
BOSTON UNIVERSITY

Printed in the United States of America
L. C. Catalog Card No. 58-12220

BOSTON UNIVERSITY PRESS
1958

BU 11-58

Contents

Preface

The four papers which form the body of this book were originally presented at the meetings of the American Political Science Association in Washington, D. C., on September 6 and 7, 1956, under the general heading of "Problems of Political Integration in Africa." The two panels devoted to this topic marked the first substantial effort to include African studies at a meeting of this character. They thus recognized the expanding concern of American scholars with developments on the continent of Africa.

The decision to publish the papers was made not only because they contribute to an understanding of the forces at work in Africa in a period of rapid change, but also because of the relative paucity of comparable material available for students of this area. The careful reconsideration and revision which the authors have given their original papers has been undertaken, therefore, not only in the light of recent developments but also to make them as useful as possible to students as well as scholars in the African field. In particular, the extensive and annotated bibliography has been prepared with both groups in mind. The volume thus has two objectives: to provide new insight into the problems of political adaptation which necessarily arise during and after the transfer of political power; and to facilitate further study of the countries with which these studies are concerned.

Warm appreciation is extended to the many people who have had a share in this volume. Professor Gabriel Almond of the 1956 program committee of the APSA helped to formulate the subject for the panels which he asked me to organize and direct. Professor William O. Brown, Director of the African Research and Studies Program, Boston University, not only gave the original impetus to publication but has contributed invaluable advice, support, and help at every stage of production. Professor Carl Rosberg of the same institution has provided many useful suggestions as well as a great deal of work in shaping the bibliographies prepared by the authors into a coordinated whole. The four authors have been unfailingly cooperative in response to the many suggestions made by the editors. A special word of thanks is due to Professor Robert Lystad who, though not an original participant on the panel, worked closely with Professor Apter in preparing the final form of the study on Ghana. The ten discussants at the two sessions of the panel — Robert Baum, Department of State; Harold Cooper, School of Advanced International Studies; Pius Okigbo, Northwestern University; Daniel McCall, Boston University; William Bascom, Northwestern University; Edward Mulcahy, Department of State; W. O. Brown, Boston University; William Diez, Rochester University; Roland Young, Northwestern University; Vernon McKay, School of Advanced International Studies — also contributed to this volume through the comments which they made on the original form of the papers. Thanks are also expressed to Professor Robert Moody, Chairman, the Board of Editors, Boston University Press, to Mrs. Mary Bull, former Research Assistant, African Studies Program, and to Mrs. Irene Bishop who has so skillfully piloted this book through the press despite the difficulties presented to any publisher by a cooperative work.

GWENDOLEN M. CARTER,
Smith College

February 1958
Northampton, Massachusetts

I

Introduction: The Process of Transition

GWENDOLEN M. CARTER, *Smith College*
WILLIAM O. BROWN, *Boston University*

The word "transition" is often used in a narrow sense to refer to the process whereby a colonial territory achieves its political independence. In this volume, the concept is given a more inclusive meaning: the evolution towards full social control of the instruments of government. This broader use of the term is justified by the fact that to establish democratic rule involves far more than the right of a people to decide on its own type of political status and external relations. This right is an essential step, of course, in the evolution towards social control for it transfers the seat of ultimate political power from external to internal instruments of government whether the territory decides to have a separate, independent existence or to adopt a new form of association with the former metropole, such as is involved in Commonwealth status. But essential as is this stage of evolution for the growth of a democratic community, it cannot of itself solve the problems of responsible use of political power. It is commonly easier, in practice, to mobilize forces in support of the transfer of power from imperial to local rule than to establish a viable political system in which the mass of the people effectively participate.

Although the emphasis in this volume is on political transition, there is full awareness that political developments constantly interact with changes in economic life, the social system, and culture. Political activities and movements in part reflect and in part give direction to ideologies and social forces which are generated by such internal factors, as well as by external influences. The political aspects of change have a particular importance, however, not only as the most obvious indications of development but also because of their impact on international relations.

Since World War II, all of colonial Africa, with the possible exception of the Portuguese territories, has experienced varying degrees and stages of political transition. Since 1951, five former dependent territories have become independent: Libya in 1951; the Republic of Tunisia, the Kingdom of Morocco, and the Republic of the Sudan in 1956; and Ghana in March 1957. There are now nine independent countries in Africa for Egypt, Ethiopia, Liberia, and the Union of South Africa have long possessed this status. The still dependent territories, particularly those under British and French rule, have also undergone substantial though not yet decisive modifications of their colonial status and relationships, and in many instances they too are already confronting within their own boundaries conflicting claims for a share in political power such as inevitably arise within an independent state.

While the studies in this volume are limited to British Africa, they deal with a striking variety of political situations. The first two studies are concerned with the most politically advanced of the British territories in West Africa: Ghana and Nigeria. The former of these countries has only recently experienced the full transfer of political power and has not yet solved the problems of providing full democratic control of the instruments of government. The latter, though already on the threshold of Commonwealth status, is still seeking constitutional means of overbridging the regional, tribal, and local divisions which stand in the way of building a viable state.

The latter two studies in the volume deal with the most complex plural societies of Central and East Africa: the Federation of Rhodesia and Nyasaland, and Kenya. Particularly in Southern Rhodesia and Kenya, the white minorities have long insisted on a predominant voice in political affairs, both because of their "rights as Englishmen," and to ensure the economic and social control which they claim is the legitimate return for the crucial contributions they have made to the development of these territories. Both in the Federation and in Kenya, however, the majority Africans have recently achieved a limited franchise and a measure of political representation. And whereas European control seems firmly entrenched in the Federation, a struggle for political power is underway in Kenya which is the more bitter because of its threat to European dominance.

Different as are these four situations, there is a common factor in the strivings by self-conscious groups within each of these communities for adequate representation or for power. A major difference is that until independence is granted, an outside and ultimately responsible imperial authority can attempt to shape the character of the constitutional structure within which the jockeying for political power takes place. But no external power can do more than provide this framework and perhaps encourage, or even dragoon intransigent elements into experimenting with it. Ultimately, whether a territory is independent, as is Ghana, or on the verge of independence, as are Nigeria and the Federation, or has its independence deliberately withheld pending more settled constitutional arrangements, as with Kenya, the decisions about the extent of democratic participation and political control must be made within the community concerned. Such decisions are always difficult. They are the more difficult in these countries since in none of them (nor indeed in any African territory) is there a strong sense of common society, or social order, which can help to resolve conflicting interests.

Since the most obvious instruments of power are political, change is commonly measured in terms of representation and executive control. These, in turn, require and thus stimulate the growth of political organization. Because the British attempt to adapt political institutions to the conditions peculiar to a given territory, and because they have supported such rapid constitutional changes since World War II, British Africa has been a veritable political laboratory during the past decade. Official majorities have been replaced by unofficial ones; legislative councils have been linked to executive responsibility; party government has developed and become increasingly effective.

The rapidity of such changes has naturally resulted in local groups and the imperial power giving particular attention to fuller representation and extension of political responsibilities. Not surprisingly, this development often places far too little emphasis on other factors no less important for democratic self-government: an impartial and well-trained civil service; and high standards for the local judiciary as the ultimate safeguard of the rule of law. Admittedly the scarcity of trained personnel, added to the limited social and political cohesion of these African territories would have made it extraordinarily difficult to meet these needs even if more attention had been given to them at an earlier date but the lacks inevitably complicate the problems of developing responsible use of political power.

Moreover, perhaps inevitably, there has been too little understanding of the essential role of the opposition in a well functioning political system. A nationalist movement or party, like, for example, the Convention People's Party in the Gold Coast, is naturally concerned far less in the period before independence with a healthy balance of political forces within parliament than with taking over power from the metropole. In Kenya, the newly elected African members see their role much less in terms of criticism in the interests of the whole community than of strengthening their own position with their constituents by appearing as the special defenders of African interests. In neither situation is there the safeguard of general community interests which a watchful, perceptive and critical opposition can provide.

All the more serious, therefore, is the tendency of the parliamentary system to lend itself to concentration of authority. Through the long processes of history, the United Kingdom has evolved a subtly balanced system of power and restraint. But when transplanted to societies in which this balance between power and restraint is lacking, or exists only to a limited degree, the parliamentary system tends towards unitary and centralized government. In Nigeria, and in the Federation of Rhodesia and Nyasaland, constitutional restraints have been inserted in response to particular features of their situation: in the former because of sharp tribal and organizational differences in the major regions; in the latter so the British can temporarily retain control over native policy in the two northern protectorates, Northern Rhodesia and Nyasaland. But in the Federation, the removal of this British control of native policy in the northern territories is an essential step for the achievement of full Commonwealth status, and when this step is taken much of the rationale behind its federal structure will disappear. In Nigeria, the achievement of independence is less dependent upon developing a strong central government than on resolving the differences between the regions but the two processes may well go together.

Generally speaking, therefore, the tendency throughout the greater part of British Africa is towards centralized and unitary government. In West Africa the strongest counter forces to this tendency are traditional and tribal. Political integration is, of course, held back by the diversity of the peoples of these territories, which has been reinforced by history, tradition, and culture. Moreover, British respect for and use of native authorities in the process of administration has often reinforced their power and prestige. In some instances this traditional authority has merged with a growing political consciousness to form what may be called "modern tribalism" in which tribal loyalty and political organization reinforce each other.

In the drive to achieve ultimate legislative and executive power, however, a wholly tribally oriented group rarely forms an effective counterpoise to a congress-type or a mass political party. The latter, as they have emerged in West Africa under the direction of an Nkrumah or Azikiwe (or in Kenya under Mboya), do not attempt to break tribal ties but rather both to use and to transcend them: to strengthen their own movement by securing tribal support and yet to develop trans-tribal links and a series of objectives which have general rather than purely tribal appeal. Such congress-type or mass political parties embody features characteristic of Western political parties but directed to their own distinctive needs. Such parties commonly owe allegiance to a dominant leader who often is their founder. They use modern techniques of propaganda and electioneering, the more so because their electorate is still largely illiterate. They are dedicated to social and economic programs aimed at improving the living standards of their people since they feel under compulsion to claim they can provide more than the colonial administrations they have replaced, or expect to replace.

At every stage of the progression to full local political control, the process of political adaptation is at work. It appears in the adjustments between colonial officials and African representatives; it is less obvious but hardly less important in the adjustments between the traditional tribal authorities and the "modern" elements who are becoming the locus of power, both at the local and national levels. Particularly subtle is the response in the minds of those who feel a continued allegiance and even awe for traditional authorities, whether chiefly or as represented by the council of elders, and who must reconcile this allegiance in practice with decision-making through the conciliar system.

No less, or perhaps even more, strain appears when colonial rule comes to an end and the national forum becomes the scene of competing interests: traditional versus modern; regional versus national; conservatives versus radicals; intellectuals, professional classes, and richer farmers versus the working class and poorer farmers; or varied coalitions or combinations of these protagonists. The very achievement of independence gives the dominant political party, or coalition, a nationalist aura which reinforces its political strength or prestige. It speaks for and claims to represent the national ideal. Criticism of its actions or programs can be labeled "anti-national," "reactionary," or even "subversive." Moreover, since the forces of integration have been on the side of the dominant party, as with the Convention People's Party in Ghana, the composition of the opposition groups tends to be varied and their interests divergent and particularistic. The weakness of the opposition and its limited capacity to develop a distinctive and positive program on national issues tend to inhibit the development of a national contest in which party interests are subordinate to national interests, and political issues are resolved within the framework of a responsible parliamentary system. Thus the interplay of political forces which create a balance in a mature parliamentary system is often lacking in a state like Ghana. Under such circumstances political adaptation is slowed and easily subject to distortion. If a situation of this type persists too long it may develop into government by a single party which tends to regard national interests as identical with its own.

While these are some of the more important problems of transition in British West Africa, the further dimension of inter-racial rivalry, if not of tension, conflict, and struggle, is added in East and Central Africa. At the moment, the concentration in the Federation of Rhodesia and Nyasaland on constitutional issues and reforms tends to veil the potential but rapidly crystallizing conflicts of interests between the dominant but numerically weak white minority and the subordinate African majority. The pressure by the European group for Commonwealth status intensifies the conflict since most African leaders assume with justification that sovereign status for the Federation will reinforce the political control and dominance of the European.

In Kenya the struggle for power, though still carried on within a constitutional framework, is becoming increasingly acute. This struggle broadly has two aspects: territorial versus imperial, and European versus African. In the past, the British Government has acted to restrain the white settlers from their goal of unfettered political power. At the moment, the colonial administration is trying to preserve a balance between the entrenched interests of the European settlers and an emergent but increasingly powerful trans-tribal mobilization and organization of Africans. It is well within the realm of possibility, however, that the British Government might feel compelled to act in the future as the protector of the European position and interests in Kenya. If this occurs, or if the power struggle along racial lines is intensified and sharpened, it might well imperil the chances for a peaceful resolution of the power issue in Kenya.

Disturbing as are some of these major trends, both in West Africa and in East and Central Africa, they should not overshadow the impressive accomplishments since World War II. Since that time the dependent Gold Coast has become the independent Dominion of Ghana; Great Britain's largest remaining colony has moved so far along the way to full self-rule that there is a strong likelihood of independence for the Federation of Nigeria by 1960 if intra-regional and inter-regional issues can be resolved. The Federation of Rhodesia and Nyasaland is at least nominally based on a concept of partnership between Europeans and Africans, which stands in sharp contrast to South Africa's policy of racial separation and European dominance. Despite critical issues in Kenya, that country has emerged from the critical period resulting from the Mau Mau rebellion into one which is characterized by an attempt to resolve through constitutional means the political and power issues which divide the races.

In the papers that follow not only the problems but also some of the achievements of this post-war period will become apparent. Tensions and conflicts are endemic in these situations of change, transition, and adaptation in Africa. Even a partial resolution of the problems inherent in such situations represents a considerable achievement.

II

Bureaucracy, Party, and Constitutional Democracy:

An examination of political role systems in Ghana*

DAVID E. APTER, *The University of Chicago*
ROBERT A. LYSTAD, *Tulane University*

INTRODUCTION AND METHOD

NATIONALISM in the British territories in Africa has resulted in a series of constitutional reforms. These have come as consequences of general patterns of development in the colonial territories. At some point in the history of the colonies an identifiable degree of coherence has emerged from the original inchoate and inarticulate antagonism to colonial administration. The perspectives of the colonials have sharpened. Their grievances have clarified, acquired solidity, and generated well-defined issues. Chiefs have realized their increasing inability to rule their districts as before. Education, commercialization, religion, urbanization, occupational specialization, all have come to exert pressures which have been subversive of both the traditional and the colonial systems and have led toward a new synthesis of political systems.

* This analysis was read at the APSA meetings in Sept. 1956 in unrevised form. This study was done in conjunction with the West African Comparative Analysis Project under a grant from the Carnegie Foundation. The authors wish to acknowledge their debt to the Foundation and to the other members of the project.

THE PATTERNS

As these patterns have developed, simple reforms on an *ad hoc* basis have tended to multiply difficulties; instead of providing permanent solutions to problems, they have come mainly to herald subsequent major constitutional advances. In response to an increasingly strong nationalist call for self-government, these advances have embodied a progressive change from emphasis upon local government and reliance upon local groups to emphasis upon a national government, national political parties, principles of representation by election, and upon decision-making by conciliar means, that is, by representative assemblies empowered to consult, advise, and legislate. These changes have been incorporated into successive interim constitutions prepared by the Colonial Office in the attempt to introduce at least a measure of stability and controlled advance in rapidly changing situations.

One of the major problems which must be faced by the writers of constitutions is to prepare a document which can be understood by the people governed under the constitution. The understanding — or lack of understanding — of the constitution by the public affects the manner in which it can be made to operate. In Africa, constitutions tend to be understood by rather narrow segments of the population for whom they are drawn, and in order to prevent this problem from hampering future development, the device of the interim constitution has been used.

This device rests upon the assumption that interim constitutions gradually establish both the procedures of constitutional government and the public's understanding of them. By the time full self-government does occur, therefore, parliamentary and administrative procedures will have become institutionalized, that is, widely understood and accepted because they have been built into the total pattern of social life. When the permanent constitution is eventually written, the public will have come to share attitudes and beliefs about government and its functions to a degree which permits the resolution of conflicts by constitutional means.

In contrast to this "gradualist" assumption is that which maintains that even the short term existence of a colonial relationship is an affront to modern day political ethics. Such a position argues for immediate self-government in colonial territories, premised on the right of a people to make its own errors and to decide in its own fashion what sort of a political system it will enjoy. That there are problems involved in this "sink or swim" approach to political democracy seems clear even to those who regard colonialism as anathema.

The British have based their colonial policy on the first alternative assumption and have directed their efforts toward the establishment of national independence via the causeway of constitutionalism. This paper will examine some of the processes used by them in developing a parliamentary system of government in the Gold Coast and will examine some of the present consequences of this policy.

The new state of Ghana, granted independence by the British on March 6, 1957, came into being after a series of interim constitutions, the last of which in 1954 had already brought full internal responsibility under a system of Cabinet Government. Public support for the Convention People's Party, the principal nationalist party, had been interpreted by the British as a clear public demand for independence. Subsequent conflict between the Convention People's Party and the Opposition over the terms of self-government was not viewed by the Colonial Office or the British Parliament as a lack of "readiness" for independence.

It is not the purpose of this paper to discuss these internal conflicts. It is sufficient to say that Ghana remains divided on many fundamental issues but that all political parties appear committed to the basic framework of constitutional democracy within which their difficulties must be resolved.

* * * * *

The method adopted for this analysis is to rank interrelated roles and membership groups in terms of their functional specificity or their functional diffuseness. These are not the only qualities of role relationships.[1] These qualities, however, are of crucial importance for the understanding of roles which have varying degrees of authority or subordination to authority vested in them. Governmental roles clearly fall within this category, although any roles which have aspects of authority may be understood more clearly and compared more readily by means of this method.

As used in this study, the terms of this method have the following meanings:

---

[1] See Marion Levy, *The Structure of Society,* Princeton University Press, 1952, for other "analytic aspects of relationship structures" and for a discussion of functional specificity and diffuseness which has served as a point of departure for the development of the method used in this paper.

Role: any identifiable position in a social relationship between two or more persons. Each role is considered as having a function to perform, a goal(s) to be achieved, a desired state of affairs to be established. In achieving its goal(s), a role makes use of certain means defined by the society as appropriate to the role. Perhaps the most familiar synonym for "role" is "office" when dealing with certain processes of government as in this study.

Membership groups: a system of interacting roles, in which there is a preponderance of shared goals and shared means to the achievement of the goals. Among the membership groups frequently referred to in this study will be the Cabinet, the Parliament, the national political party, the parliamentary party, the party bureaucracy, the civil service government bureaucracy, and the public. As the study will make clear, membership groups within membership groups must also be distinguished because of the degrees of difference which emerge with respect either to goals or the means to goals.

Functional specificity and functional diffuseness: the qualities of goals, and means to goals, which characterize different roles and membership groups. "Specific" and "diffuse" represent the two poles of characteristic role action between which varying degrees of specificity or diffuseness may be differentiated. Degrees between the poles are designated as predominantly specific, specific-diffuse, and predominantly diffuse.

Ranking: determination of the degree of specificity or diffuseness characteristic of the action of a role or of a membership group. The system of ranking uses three sets of criteria stated in terms of polar variables. Both the goals and the means of each role or membership group are ranked on the following bases:

a. Required goal(s), mean(s) — Alternative goal(s), mean(s).
b. Explicit goal(s), mean(s) — Implicit goal(s), mean(s).
c. Narrow scope goal(s), mean(s)—Wide scope goal(s), mean(s).

These polar terms are used as follows:

a. Required: without alternative goal(s), mean(s).
   Alternative: the role or membership group enjoys a choice of goal(s), mean(s), any one of which is considered equally desirable or valid.
b. Explicit: clearly defined criteria for goal(s), mean(s).
   Implicit: vaguely defined criteria for goal(s), mean(s).

c. Scope: range within which the goal(s), mean(s) have effect. The scope of a role or membership group is judged as being narrow or wide.

The technique used in ranking is as follows:

A score of "1" is given for each of the polar variables to the left; a score of "0" is given for each of the polar variables to the right.

A functionally specific role or membership group would have a score of "6" (goals: required "1", explicit "1", narrow "1"; means: required "1", explicit "1", narrow "1").

A functionally diffuse role or membership group would have a score of "0" (goals: alternative "0", implicit "0"; wide "0"; means: alternative "0", implicit "0", wide "0").

The complete set of terms used in ranking functional specificity or diffuseness is as follows:

Specific (Score 6)
Predominantly specific (Score 5 or Score 4)
Specific-diffuse (Score 3)
Predominantly diffuse (Score 2 or Score 1)
Diffuse (Score 0)

Throughout this paper the adverb "functionally" will be omitted, but it is to be implied in each case.

The Origins of Ghana Constitutionalism in the Civil Service

The Gold Coast was first ruled by a colonial administration in which administrators in the Colonial Service were responsible to the British Parliament through the Colonial Office. During the years prior to 1957 many of the administrative roles came to be filled by Africans. The administration today is conducted by the Ghana Civil Service responsible to the Ghana Parliament through the Prime Minister.

In its internal structure the colonial administration is specific in nature (Score 6; goals: required, explicit, narrow; means: required, explicit, narrow). This is characteristic of bureaucracies generally. They involve a complexly organized hierarchy of clearly defined roles, an elaborate set of rules, and they place a heavy emphasis on administrative efficiency toward achievement of well-defined goals. In its relationship with the public, however, the colonial administration is predominantly diffuse (Score 1; goals: required, implicit, wide; means: alternative, implicit, wide). It enjoys wide latitude in its authoritative decision-making and in the scope of its effect on the public. The reason for this difference in scores is that the diffuse policy-making roles and the specific, bureaucratic, policy-implementing roles are parts of a single membership group, the colonial administration; frequently both types of roles are filled by a single person alternating between them. In stable, democratic governments the bureaucracy has no direct relationship with the public and is solely specific in its relationship with policy-making groups.

Within the colonial administration itself, particular roles vary in their degrees of specificity or diffuseness. In their relationship to other roles in the administration, such roles as Governor, Colonial Secretary, and Financial Secretary are diffuse (Score 0), while the role of District Officer is predominantly specific (Score 4; goals: required, implicit, narrow; means: required, implicit, narrow). In their relationship to the public the roles of Governor, Colonial Secretary, and Financial Secretary are also diffuse (Score 0). In its relationship to the public, however, the role of the District Officer becomes predominantly diffuse (Score 2; goals: required, implicit, wide; means: required, implicit, wide) because of the high degree of discretionary power placed in his hands. Within the colonial administration the District Officer has relatively little authority, but in relation to the public his role has a relatively high degree of authority and is characterized, therefore, by a greater degree of diffuseness. The area he administers depends upon him for many of the important decisions by which the structure of traditional society is altered.

Due to the immediacy of this role relationship and the degree of discretion permitted the District Officer during the earlier years of colonial administration in the Gold Coast, the District Officer was often more important than most of his colleagues in the Secretariat. Upon this role depended the actual functioning of the colonial government, the maintenance of an orderly legal framework of political life, the improvement of health and sanitation, the collection of taxes, and the enforcement of other financial regulations depending upon the economic and financial status of the territory under its jurisdiction. The scope of the District Officer's authority widened as the colonial administration widened its interests to include education, agriculture, forestry, husbandry, mining, commerce, and other activities.

Africans entered into the colonial administrative system at the level of the most specific roles. In performing his role, the District Officer made use of chiefs and native authorities, both groups being specific in nature (Score 6) in contrast to his predominantly diffuse role (Score 2). Elsewhere in the system Africans gradually came to be employed as clerks and police (Score 6).

Except in certain individual cases, the concerted efforts of the early nationalistic movements to fill the more diffuse, more authoritative roles higher in the administration met with British opposition. To the British, colonial administration in the classic pattern was unthinkable with a corps of locally recruited people, and, of course, in the early period few Africans could meet the educational standards of recruitment. But even when a group of professionally qualified Africans gradually developed, they were generally barred from entrance into the more diffuse, more authoritative roles in the civil service.

Nationalism, in its early phases, directed itself as much to this problem of Africanization of the existing colonial administration as to the more fundamental problem of the right of a colonial administration to rule. Blocked by British opposition to rapid, indiscriminate Africanization, nationalists began to demand the establishment of membership groups which had at least local advisory status, a demand toward which the British were favorable. In theory, at least, these groups were specific (Score 6), being severely delimited and restricted in scope of authority; in practice, however, they came to perform in a somewhat more diffuse, authoritative manner as educated politicians assumed more and more of the roles once vested in traditional leaders. Nationalists came to dominate territorial councils and town councils. Eventually they became members of the Gold Coast Legislative Council, partly as a result of their own efforts, partly as the result of changes in colonial administrative practice. Until 1951 this Council was the most authoritative conciliar body in the Gold Coast, although it remained predominantly specific in nature (Score 4; goals: alternative, explicit, narrow; means: alternative, explicit, narrow) because of its largely advisory status.

Nationalism, in the radical phase opened by the Convention People's Party (CPP), was little concerned with the gradual widening of participation in politics by a conservative African elite. It demanded that absolute control of all political membership groups and roles, diffuse and specific, be given to Africans without any responsibility to such a higher, diffuse, authoritative group as the British Parliament. Although it upheld the creation of a completely independent, diffuse, parliamentary authority within Ghana as its fundamental objective, the CPP also recognized that government requires a dependent, specific, civil service bureaucracy to carry out the tasks assigned to it by the parliament. The CPP stressed, therefore, the maintenance of the civil service with a clear understanding of its specific role in the governing of an independent state.

In summary, early nationalism appeared content to play roles and to support membership groups which were specific or, at the most, predominantly specific in character, because their primary relationship was with the diffuse, authoritative British Parliament through the Colonial Office. The radical nationalism of the CPP made clear it would be content only if it controlled all the governmental roles and membership groups, free from any responsibility to the British Parliament.

The transition from the Gold Coast as a colony to Ghana as an independent constitutional democracy required a change in the qualities of the roles and membership groups within the government. Under the British the colonial administration was specific in its internal organization, diffuse in its relationship with the public. In the absence of any representative, conciliar assemblies, there was no real differentiation between administrative and policy-making groups. In relationship to the public these actually comprised a single, diffuse group with both specific and diffuse aspects. Being manned only by Europeans and moreover being exclusive in its standards of recruitment and behavior, the colonial administration provided a focal point at which to direct public antagonism.

Once the CPP was granted increasing degrees of authority, however, it recognized how much its performance depended upon the colonial administration in its specific aspects. With nothing less than control of all roles, specific and diffuse, as its goal, the CPP came to differentiate sharply between the administrative and the policy-making membership groups within government. It regarded the conciliar groups as properly diffuse, the civil service administrative groups as properly specific; the conciliar groups were to ascertain public needs and demands and to put them into the form of orders and legislation which were then to be carried out by the civil service administrative groups.

The progressive changes under the interim constitutions allowed for this differentiation between policy-making and policy-implementing groups during the transitional period when the CPP was given effective internal authority within the Gold Coast. Its consequence was to keep government operating at a high level of efficiency while new ministers and legislators became familiar with the procedures and canons of government.[2]

The relationship between the specific, bureaucratic membership groups and the diffuse, conciliar or representative membership groups in government is the most crucial one in modern constitutionalism. Development of a harmonious relationship between them poses difficult problems in a colonial territory which is moving toward self-government, because the bureaucratic groups, in the form of the colonial administration, have long been functioning, whereas the conciliar groups are just coming into being.[3] The conciliar groups are composed, furthermore, of politicians, trained in the rough and tumble of independence-movement politics, far removed from the setting which prepared British administrators to move with ease between specific, bureaucratic roles and diffuse, parliamentary roles.

During the transition period of the interim constitutions, while Africans were achieving genuine political authority in such conciliar bodies as the Cabinet and the Legislature, heavy reliance was placed upon bureaucratic roles for guidance. The Permanent Secretaries, civil service roles filled exclusively by British personnel, provided information at Cabinet meetings, prepared politically feasible alternatives for the Ministers to propose in Parliament when problems arose, and sat in the spectators' gallery during sessions of the Legislative Assembly in order to give support to their African seniors. It was hoped, furthermore, that the Permanent Secretaries could introduce into both the Cabinet and the

[2] This statement does not imply a clear-cut distinction between "politics and administration." Nevertheless the subordinate position of administrative roles and groups is a characteristic of the system. The very term "civil servant" is an expression of this position. During the last stages of British rule, the civil service was able to maintain a dominant or "mentor" position while remaining constitutionally and functionally subordinate.

[3] This was not the case in the Western world, where bureaucracy and conciliarism developed simultaneously in keeping with a pattern of cultural and structural changes pervasive throughout the societies. Here bureaucracy and conciliarism shared some of the same characteristics: a mutual subordination to principles of government shared with the public, a pattern of the division of labor and the division of power, a concept of the public interest, means of determining the public interest, etc. Bureaucracy was not dissociated from the general social organization, and it changed along with changes in public beliefs. Bureaucratic units do have their own sub-cultures, but these are not incompatible with other sub-cultures in the society, however different they may be.

Legislature the awareness and the practice of such bureaucratic concepts as the integrity and responsibility of the group, efficiency, division and specialization of function, coordination, recognition of hierarchy and authority, and rational decision-making.

There is evidence of the success of these attempts in the way in which the CPP has relegated to unimportant roles or even denied candidacy to certain politicians who have seemed unable to work under the framework of constitutionalism. It is not yet certain, however, that the diffuse membership groupings in Ghana's political system fully comprehend the nature of the relationship between each other and between them and the specific, bureaucratic groups in the government.

The Convention People's Party

The task of a nationalist movement in a colonial territory such as the Gold Goast is a complex and difficult one. It must determine the means for uniting numerous, separate, traditional societies, each with its own history, loyalties, and vested interests, into a single, cohesive group. To do so it must provide a wide range of satisfactions to widely differing groups of people possessed of many types of social organization. In addition a nationalist movement must continue to expand. It requires increasing power and resources. As a consequence of its difficult task, it postpones the attempt to reconcile the requirements of its own existence with the requirements of socially responsible action. But eventually this reconciliation must be attempted, and this is done at that point where members of the nationalist movement begin to analyze the roles they have been playing and the roles they must play if they are to provide responsible government.

In its initial phases, a nationalist movement is predominantly a diffuse group (Score 1; goals: required, implicit, wide; means: alternative, implicit, wide). But as it begins to take form, it tends to become more and more specific. When it becomes sufficiently specific to function as a "party," it has developed a corps of functionaries, regionally and nationally identified as "patriots." Some of these may have undergone "suffering," as in the case of Ghana's "Prison Graduates." Their loyalty is to the party, and they form the basis of a stable party organization.

Party funds become subject to accounting, and financial laxity, which in the Gold Coast was a characteristic of the nationalist movement, declines. The roles of party officials become more clarified, regularized, and specialized. The leadership must become expert in propaganda and education, in organizational techniques, in mass persuasion; its "thinkers" must find popular issues and phrase them in popular terms. The growing division of labor extends downward to the activation of such roles as "vote organizers," and hierarchies of control on national, regional, district, and local levels, both rural and municipal, come into being.

Within this increasingly specific party framework, leaders emerge. They are frequently men who have displayed superior skill in specific roles but who also appear qualified to play more diffuse roles at the organizational top of the party. Just as there are differences in degrees of specificity and diffuseness between roles within the colonial administration, so are there differences between roles within the internal structure of a political party.

The most diffuse, the most authoritative of these may be called "all-purpose roles." Within the party, these roles and the persons filling them serve as sources rather than as executors of power and policy; they are superior in position to roles of a more specific nature and to those persons who fill them. Such all-purpose roles select the goals and the means for achieving them, they make explicit the nature of the goals and the means, and their range of influence is wide (Score 0). They stand in contrast to the lesser degree of discretionary power permitted to the persons in the more specific, bureaucratic roles within the party. Whereas the bureaucratic roles in the party minimize the effects of the personality of the person playing the role by clearly defining the boundaries of action, the all-purpose roles permit much greater expression of the personality of their occupants.

Similar, diffuse all-purpose roles are found both in the Parliament and in the Cabinet. Because the civil service bureaucracy is controlled by the Cabinet, furthermore, the all-purpose roles in the Cabinet may also be regarded as all-purpose roles in the civil service.

In Ghana the persons filling the all-purpose roles of the CPP also fill the all-purpose roles in the Parliament, in the Cabinet, and, therefore, in the civil service, and herein lies one of the difficult problems that must be solved before democratic government in Ghana can become meaningful. The problem may be stated in this way: In a situation in which the all-purpose roles in both the government and the political party are filled by the same persons, can the occupants effectively distinguish between their roles in the two membership groups in which they function simultaneously? The questions may be more specifically phrased in this fashion: Is the CPP to be regarded as identical with Ghana? Is constitutional government to be regarded simply as the expression of the government structure of the CPP? Is the diffuse, all-purpose role of the Life-Chairman of the CPP, Kwame Nkrumah, indistinguishable from the diffuse, all-purpose role of the Prime Minister, Kwame Nkrumah? Is Ghana in fact a one-party state?

For some members of the CPP the answers to these questions seem to be affirmative, though it is probable that most party members are unsure. It is partly in fear of an ultimate affirmative answer that the National Liberation Movement has developed in Ashanti. Depending upon its as yet unconvincing answers to these questions, the CPP either will usurp to itself alone the right to speak in the name of Ghana, or it will accept its obligation to claim authority only on the basis of victory in elections conducted under the terms of the constitution.

If the former alternative is chosen, Ghana government under the CPP will be indistinguishable in its functional qualities from the Gold Coast under colonial administration. In its internal structure it will be specific in nature (Score 6); in its relationship with the public it will be predominantly diffuse (Score 1). And it will have failed to solve the problem, present in all constitutional democracies, of the crucial relationship between specific bureaucratic groups and diffuse conciliar groups. It will have failed because in practice the role occupants failed adequately to distinguish between their roles.

The Conciliar System

During the period of the interim constitutions, the Gold Coast Government established several types of conciliar systems, that is, systems of representative assemblies established to debate, advise, or legislate. Those concerned with local government are outside the scope of this discussion, but those concerned with the central government are crucial. They comprise the legislative system.

Insofar as African participation is concerned, the change in the functional qualities of the legislative system has been a change from specific to diffuse groups and roles, from solely advisory African groups and roles to completely responsible African groups and roles. At first the Legislative

Council was primarily composed of official members, that is, individuals from the higher ranks of the Colonial Service. Gradually its membership was supplemented by unofficial members, both African and European, until in 1946 a majority of the Legislative Council members was African. In the constitutional revision of 1950 a Cabinet system was established. At that time a single political party, the CPP, became the parliamentary party which organized and controlled the predominantly African Legislative Assembly and filled all of the Cabinet roles except for three *ex-officio* British members. In the constitutional revision of 1954 the Cabinet became all-African, although the parliamentary system remained responsible to the British Parliament through the Colonial Office. On March 6, 1957, the parliamentary system assumed full responsibility for the affairs of Ghana.

THE LEGISLATURE

The device of the interim constitution has accomplished a remarkably smooth transition, in certain respects at least, from African participation in specific advisory or clerical groups to diffuse authoritative groups. In the early period of the Legislative Council the official members, most of them senior in the Colonial Service, set the procedural patterns for parliamentary operations, and the Africans who were subsequently elected or appointed to the Council accepted the patterns. Many of the Africans, furthermore, had enjoyed previous training in the civil service or in specific conciliar groups like the municipal authorities in local government. Even after 1946, when the Legislative Council had an African majority, high procedural standards prevailed.

After 1951, when a much more popularly elected Legislative Assembly came into being, the standards of debate dropped somewhat, but the conduct of the Assembly continued to conform to the rules of "the dignity of the House." And even the misconceptions, misunderstandings, errors, and sheer prejudice revealed both in committees and in open debate could not obscure the obvious seriousness of purpose manifested by the legislators. If parliamentary propriety was occasionally abused, rarely were the offenders responsible members of the government. These standards of propriety have continued down to the present.

The legislature is the fount of political authority in constitutional government (Score 0). Whether or not it has achieved this status in Ghana is as yet uncertain. The Opposition charges that Nkrumah and the CPP do not differentiate between themselves and the legislature, and the Government replies that the Opposition is without faith in the constitution. It is still possible to say, however, that despite the depth of feeling on constitutional matters and despite the degree to which the Government and the Opposition have been driven apart, they both appear to be committed to parliamentary supremacy in principle and to oppose overt identification of a political party with the legislature.

THE CPP PARLIAMENTARY PARTY

Since the CPP as the dominant party organizes and controls the Parliament, an analysis of its structure as it functions in the Parliament is essential to the understanding of the Ghana conciliar system.

In the internal structure of the CPP a differentiation has developed between the role of "delegate" and the role of "representative." With respect to the qualitative aspects of these roles in their relationship with the parliamentary party, the delegate is specific (Score 6), the representative is specific-diffuse (Score 3; goals: required, implicit, narrow; means: alternative, implicit, narrow).

Persons playing the role of delegate are persons, usually without special talents, who are completely responsive to the demands of their public constituencies. Because of this strong public support, they can be used by the CPP to state the popular issues and to announce the CPP position on them. Ordinarily they are firm in their adherence to CPP discipline. Persons playing the role of representative are less responsive to the demands of their constituents, more directed by their own discretion or "conscience," and capable of non-conformity to CPP discipline, even though actual non-conformity is rare. If either delegate or representative behaves too independently, an attempt is made to remove him from politics. If, however, the delegate is too powerfully supported by his public constituency, he may be incorporated into the Cabinet or into the policy-making group within the CPP. The non-conforming representative may either be removed from politics or appointed to a specific, non-authoritative role in some government agency such as a marketing board.

Delegates of special interest groups, such as a trade union, a voluntary association, or a trading association, tend to enact the role of representative on matters not pertinent to their special interest. The importance of these delegates in matters of national significance, however, is relatively minor.[4]

In addition to the roles of delegate and representative, a third role, that of the "party core," has been differentiated. It is a predominantly specific role, similar to that of the delegate, though different in its content. The person filling this role is regarded as qualified for Parliament primarily because of his effective service to the CPP. He is a hero to his constituency, which accepts rather than determines his actions. His actions, in turn, are determined by the CPP, to which he is loyal both inside and outside of Parliament. As a group, the party core is in closest touch with the CPP bureaucracy, and individuals may actually be members of the party bureaucracy. If they show a tendency toward non-conformity to CPP discipline, they are dropped, but if in addition to complete reliability they are intelligent, are effective organizers, have strong, independent backing, or are in any way crucial to success either in government or within the party, they may be appointed as Government Whips or given other responsible tasks in the government.

Within the parliamentary party these roles are combined to form the "back bench," a membership group which, in its relationship with the CPP, is predominantly specific in nature (Score 4; goals: required, explicit, wide; means: required, explicit, wide).

A fourth role which must be distinguished in the parliamentary party is that of the Ministerial Secretary, a particularly complex role because of the position it holds with respect both to the more diffuse role of the Minister, to which it is subordinate, and to the more specific roles and membership groups over which it can exert its dominance. Among the latter roles and membership groups are the CPP, the back bench of the parliamentary party, the Parliament itself, and the civil service bureaucracy.

In its relationship with the role of Minister, that of the Ministerial Secretary is, in theory, specific (Score 6). When, however, the person filling this role is better trained and possessed of a more deft sense of judgment than his superior, the Minister, his role may in actuality become as predominantly diffuse as that of the Minister. In such cases, his role may possess considerable power to make decisions, even though

[4] An exception to this generalization are the Trade Union Congress representatives who are assuming an increasingly important and aggressive role in their constituencies and in the union organizations themselves.

it is a delegated rather than an official power. When the Minister is himself a person of ability or power, the role of Ministerial Secretary may require simply the performance of routine, clerical tasks.

In its relationship with the back bench of the parliamentary party, this role is more diffuse. The Ministerial Secretary is frequently a person who has performed well in some other specific capacity in the CPP or in the government. In this case he may become useful as a communicator between his Minister or the Cabinet and the back bench as a determiner of back bench action. His relationship with the more specific roles within the CPP is similar to that with the back bench, as is his relationship with the civil service. But in all of these relationships (and this is characteristic of the more diffuse roles in any relationship), the personality of the role occupant affects the function of the role. He may range from a highly responsible figure, being groomed for future office, to a much more irresponsible, self-seeking figure, who may attempt to exploit his political following on the back bench and in the political party by dispensing political patronage.

This complex role is important, furthermore, in that it is the principal means by which the relationship between the civil service bureaucracy and the Parliament is regulated. The English rules governing access by Members of Parliament to civil service administrators have been retained in Ghana. These rules are reflected in a statement by Professor Robson: ". . . the dangers of a too close relationship between Members of Parliament and civil servants might be considerable. A civil servant might be deflected by political influence of an MP or a group of MP's. He might be made to feel that his own future depended to some extent on the favour or disfavour in which he stood with members of the legislature. A Minister's authority in his department might be undermined by legislative support for a particular division or branch."[5] Standing as it does between the Member of Parliament and the Minister, the role of the Ministerial Secretary provides its occupant with considerable discretionary power to determine who may and who may not approach the Minister or any of the civil servants in his department. According to the rules, there is no other legitimate access to the civil servant except through his Minister, and the Ministerial Secretary

---

[5] See Robson, Wlliam A. (Editor), *The Civil Service in England and France,* London, The Hogarth Press, 1956, Chapter 1, page 10.

guards that approach. It may also be pointed out that the opportunity for corruption at this diffuse level of authority is considerable.

The final membership group, or system or roles to be distinguished in the parliamentary party is that of the "front bench." It is comprised of the Ministers and the Prime Minister, and it is a diffuse group in all its relationships (Score 0). Certain of the Ministries which dispense patronage, such as the Ministry of Works, may be more specific in nature than others. Certain of the Ministers in the front bench, furthermore, may also play such predominantly specific roles as "party core" or technically competent "administrators." But the group itself is diffuse in its relationships with all other roles and groups.

It is through the front bench that the civil service must exert its influence. It is the front bench which gives the entire Ghana Parliament its vitality by demanding proper parliamentary behavior from the members of the parliamentary party. It is the front bench which exerts great control over the CPP itself and which is associated with the Prime Minister in his role as political party leader.

Within the front bench, the most important, the most authoritative Ministers play "all-purpose" roles. They have a prestige and a position which allows them considerable personal latitude in the exercise of discretion. In their role they are capable of combining the characteristics of the party core and the technical expert. In addition, the persons occupying these all-purpose roles — of whom the Prime Minister, Kwame Nkrumah, the Minister of Finance, K. A. Gbedemah, and the Minister of Interior (1957), Krobo Edusei, are outstanding examples — possess personalities which give them a symbolic position in the conciliar system and in the entire nation.

In their special relationship with the public, these men in their all-purpose roles function as symbols for the nation — as do all political leaders of great stature — and they need no justification for their actions other than their own symbolic positions. It is as public symbols that these men, in their most diffuse, all-purpose roles in the political party, in the parliamentary party, and in the Parliament, can serve either to strengthen or weaken the patterns of constitutional government in Ghana.

THE CABINET

In its relationship with the parliamentary party, the Cabinet, comprised of the Ministerial roles, is a diffuse membership group. But the

Cabinet is a complex group which also has relationships with the civil service bureaucracy, Parliament, and with the political party. Each of these requires analysis.

In its relationship with the civil service bureaucracy, the Cabinet is a predominantly specific group (Score 4; goals: required, explicit, wide; means: required, explicit, wide). It is, however, more diffuse than is the civil service itself, for the Cabinet is the most authoritative part of the civil service. In this relationship the civil service is specific, since the scope of its goals and means is narrower than that of the Cabinet, the Ministers of which are responsible heads of the departments of the civil service. In his capacity as head of a department, the Cabinet Minister is a specialist in local government, housing, education, and the like, of whom efficient performance is required. In order to achieve his goals, he must share in certain respects the perspectives and skills of the senior civil service personnel and must have an understanding of the operations and procedures of the bureaucratic department for which he is responsible.

During the period of the interim constitutions, the Ministers learned the requirements of their roles in their civil service relationships from the British Permanent Secretaries, who not only continued their former specialist roles but also served as "mentors" to the Ministers under whom they worked. So important was this latter function that often the qualities of the roles were reversed, the Ministerial role being more specific than that of the Permanent Secretary. Despite the occasional complaint that a Minister was hampered by his Permanent Secretary, the strikingly effective record of successive Gold Coast Cabinets during the interim period is one indication of the success of this "training period." Cabinet Ministers were enabled by this device to approach decisions with the necessary information and criteria for judgment.

The ministerial skills developed through this relationship with the civil service also served to establish the Cabinet as a diffuse group in its relationship with Parliament and to make possible a high standard of procedures in that body. The Minister, equipped with information and experience in decision-making which Members of Parliament did not possess, was frequently able to control and even to intimidate his less knowledgeable party colleagues and the Opposition.

The relationship of the Cabinet with the political party demonstrates the complexity and difficulty of the Minister's role. With respect to many issues, of course, the Cabinet is diffuse and the political party specific, for the Ministers possess not only technical skills but also the symbolic position of recognized leadership which other party members do not possess in equal degree. But on many issues and over a long time-span, the Cabinet as a group and each Minister individually must be responsive to the party, for without party support and the public support which it represents, the Cabinet fails. In this aspect of the Cabinet's relationship with the political party, therefore, the Cabinet is specific-diffuse (Score 3; goals: required, explicit, narrow; means: alternative, implicit, wide). The Cabinet retains sufficient diffuseness to determine the means to goals, but the political party defines the goals themselves. The Cabinet Minister must remain a party politician; he must cater to his party membership. Some of the latter, in fact, have been brought into the Parliament and the Cabinet, where they play, among their other roles, the role of party core.

Because of the nature of its relationships with all of these groups, the Cabinet serves as the principal integrator of governmental and political party groups. The person who fills the role of Minister, therefore, must be capable of finding the means to balance these groups; he must have parliamentary agility, political shrewdness, judgment and sagacity and, above all, he requires the ability to combine in himself all the alternative roles which he, as Minister, must play as leader of his civil service department, as party politician, as parliamentarian, as leader of the parliamentary party, and as public symbol. He must be able to integrate all other political roles and groups and to do so in such a way as to strengthen his role and his own position in it.

It has been pointed out above that during the period of the interim constitutions, the Cabinet was diffuse in its relationship with Parliament primarily because of its superior knowledge and experience in decision-making gained through the training provided by the British members of the senior civil service. This is not the relationship characteristic of constitutional democracies. In this system of government, the Cabinet provides leadership for the parliamentary party, for the public, and for the civil service bureaucracy, but it is subordinate to Parliament to which it is responsible. In the ideal relationship, therefore, it is Parliament which is the diffuse group, the Cabinet which is specific.

The Ghana Parliament has not yet assumed this essential control over the Cabinet, and it will be unable to do so as long as the Opposition remains comparatively ineffective. The distinctions between the civil service bureaucracy, the parliamentary party, the Cabinet, Parliament, and the political party have not yet been clearly defined. It is not that the roles have been poorly filled. Radical-populist as the CPP is, it has selected leaders for Cabinet positions who, for the most part, are men with higher educations, with old school ties, and with experience in other cultures. They have effectively played their roles. Some of them are fully as technically skilled as the African specialists who fill specific roles in the higher ranks of the civil service. As nationalist leaders they have achieved their nationalist goals. In the Cabinet they have succeeded in reconciling the different relationships of their role in such a way as to provide effective leadership acceptable to the public.

But the question of the Cabinet's relationship to Parliament remains unanswered. If the political party regards itself as the government of Ghana, then the Cabinet is only a device to cloak authority in constitutional garb. If the party differentiates clearly between itself and the government, then the Cabinet will become subordinate to Parliament, and this essential requirement of constitutional democracy will be met.

Role Integration and Authority

The significant roles and membership groups and the complex network of relationships between them which have arisen under the policy of interim constitutions have now been analyzed. The assumption on which this policy has been based is that gradual, progressive devolution of authority to Africans provides the time and experience necessary for coming to understand and to institutionalize the patterns of constitutional democracy. Has this assumption as yet been justified?

In many respects, the transition from colonial administration to constitutional self-government has enjoyed marked success, and the foregoing analysis indicates those areas. A sufficient degree of integration between the roles and the membership groups has been achieved to enable the government to function without breakdown. The system has succeeded in filling the crucial political roles with men of technical skill who also possess the qualities of leadership. The policy, furthermore, has succeeded in gaining public acceptance of certain of the values of a constitutional democracy: the public has come to accept the new political roles which are part of the constitutional system; and they have come increasingly to rely upon the constitutional means of political action available to the public in the vote, in petitions and memorials, etc. In keeping with the goal of the policy of interim constitutions, therefore, two types of authoritative political membership groups, broadly defined, have in fact been developed: these two groups are comprised of the political elite, those with authority in the governmental system, and the public, that group whose support is necessary in order to maintain the elite in their positions.

In order effectively to capture and use the authority of the public group, political parties develop their own bureaucracies. When governmental political roles (previously unavailable to Africans or filled by the politically conservative African elite representative of the earliest stages of nationalism) become open, the nationalist party tends to fill them only from among the leaders of the party itself. The party also develops specialists in organization, propaganda, communications, tactics, and strategy. In so doing a twofold differentiation of function emerges: certain roles come to be regarded as specialist, others as all-purpose. The specialist roles are integrated into a true party bureaucracy; the all-purpose roles supply legitimacy and leadership for the bureaucracy, which then is regarded as subordinate to the all-purpose roles.

Ghana's political system has thus come to include two types of bureaucracy: a political party bureaucracy, and a government civil service bureaucracy. In both their internal structure and in their relationships to the groups to which they are responsible — the government bureaucracy being responsible to Parliament through the Cabinet, the party bureaucracy responsible to the party leadership — these two bureaucracies have identical qualities: they are both specific (Score 6). Both of them, furthermore, have relationships with the same two membership groups within the government, Parliament and the Cabinet, both of which are diffuse (Score 0) in these relationships. In their interaction with these membership groups, however, the goals of the two bureaucracies are quite different. The goal of the party bureaucracy is to strengthen its own position, and it tends to view Parliament and the Cabinet as groups to be manipulated in order to gain its goal. The goal of the government bureaucracy, on the other hand, is to provide effective government, and it tends to view Parliament and the Cabinet as groups which may restrict its attempts to improve government and, therefore, as groups which threaten the status of the bureaucracy itself.

The two bureaucracies do not interact directly with each other but do so indirectly through their mutual relationships with Parliament and the Cabinet.

An important tentative conclusion emerges at this point of the analysis. *The party bureaucracy and the government bureaucracy exert opposing pressures upon those persons filling all-purpose roles in Parliament and the Cabinet.*

The logic which underlies this conclusion is as follows: 1. With the formalization of constitutional practice, both bureaucracies become more developed in order to achieve their respective goals. 2. With the development of the bureaucracies, the specialist roles are differentiated more precisely; they become more specific in quality. 3. The more specific a role becomes, the more the role occupant comes to view his own narrow membership group as most crucial to the entire system. 4. The more the role occupant acts in terms of his own group, the more he seeks to avoid threats to his group, regardless of the consequences of his action for constitutional development or abstract political values.

Both bureaucracies, therefore, exert opposing pressures upon Parliament and the Cabinet in order to assure achievement of their own goals. Some CPP bureaucrats regard the government ideally as a simple reflection of the party. Some government bureaucrats regard the government ideally as a simple reflection of the civil service — viewpoint reinforced during the period of interim training under the British — and most of those who have been disappointed by political developments to the contrary have resigned, retired, or been transferred.

If the goals of the two bureaucracies differ, the means at their disposal also differ, because they stand in different relationships to the public, that basic authority group to which both are ultimately responsible in a constitutional democracy. In this relationship the government bureaucracy is specific (Score 6). The government bureaucracy has specifically defined responsibilities; it is a dependent group, specifically responsible to Parliament through the Cabinet; it operates under a formal, constitutional mandate which removes it from any direct relationship with the public. The party bureaucracy, on the other hand, has only diffusely defined responsibilities: it is an autonomous group, responsible to the party; it operates only under an informal mandate, that of public approval and allegiance. Both bureaucracies have real sources of power. Each possesses advantages which the other does not. And each, with the different means at its disposal, seeks to affect the way in which government will develop by attempting to maximize its control over Parliament and the Cabinet.

The pressures exerted by both of these bureaucracies are directed primarily toward those members of Parliament and the Cabinet who play the most important all-purpose roles. Nkrumah recognizes that his continuance in office is in part dependent upon the specialist roles in the party bureaucracy which are necessary to capture and maintain public allegiance. But he equally recognizes that his continuance in office is in part dependent upon the specialist roles in the government bureaucracy which are necessary to carry out the policies of his government and thus enable him to wage an effective campaign before the public. This latter dependence is even greater in an under-developed area like Ghana, where governmental rather than non-governmental groups are directly involved in a high proportion of the social and economic institutions of the country.

One of the major goals of the Prime Minister, the Cabinet, and the parliamentary party, therefore, is to maximize the utility of the two bureaucracies and to minimize the conflict between them.[6] This is, perhaps, one of the features of the parliamentary system in Ghana which distinguishes it from the more stabilized parliamentary systems in Europe. It gains its peculiar importance from the fact that both the Cabinet and Parliament are comprised of numerous persons who must play overlapping, diffuse roles; that is, they simultaneously hold analogous positions of authority in two theoretically and ideally separate political membership groups. The Cabinet and the front bench of the parliamentary party consists of the same individuals who are the authoritative leaders of the political party and, hence, of the party bureaucracy. On the back bench of the parliamentary party are found the roles of "delegate" and "party core," both of which conform in their actions to the party bureaucracy; indeed, the party core is made up of some of the more important party bureaucrats. The overlapping between political party roles and parliamentary roles is thus considerable.

The overlap of roles in the Cabinet has a different but analogous

[6] It must be emphasized that the conflict is an indirect one. It rarely becomes overt, although it may do so through the entrance into the conflict of another political party, such as the National Liberation Movement, which may deliberately point up the existence of opposing pressures.

pattern. Here the Cabinet members simultaneously play diffuse roles in the civil service government bureaucracy, in the parliamentary party, to which the government bureaucracy is responsible, and in the political party. Ideally, the Cabinet Minister judges the proposals of the government bureaucracy solely on the criteria of logicality and governmental efficiency, but often his overlapping roles of parliamentary party member or of political party leader prevail, and judgments are made on the criteria of what is considered politically feasible or utilitarian by the party bureaucracy.

Nkrumah's ability to maximize the utility of both bureaucracies and to minimize the conflict between them has depended until now upon his peculiar all-purpose role, a role possibly filled also by Gbedemah and Edusei. This type of role differs from overlapping roles in that the latter consist of several separate, well-defined roles which may successively or alternately be filled by the individual playing each. The all-purpose role is much more diffuse in its definition and permits the individual playing it great freedom of action, including domination of any of the overlapping roles in the bureaucracies and in Parliament. Authority for this role derives from the public, whose complete acceptance gives it a symbolic quality enjoyed by no other role. It is in this role that Nkrumah has thus far successfully maintained both his own position and an effective political system in Ghana.

The question of whether or not he can continue to do so gives rise to a second tentative conclusion: *The parliamentary system permits leaders to fill overlapping roles only; all-purpose roles, therefore, are gradually abolished.* The symbolic status of a leader declines, and he becomes the occupant of several, well-defined, specialist roles.

Nkrumah's symbolic position has already undergone such a decline. One measure of this is the revived symbolic position of chiefs, whose role in the traditional society approached that of an all-purpose role. There are many reasons for Nkrumah's apparent decline — though he remains the most significant and powerful individual in Ghana — but the most far-reaching reason is the nature of the parliamentary system itself. Once it becomes stabilized or institutionalized, this system does not permit the existence of all-purpose roles.

The logic which underlies this conclusion is as follows:

1. As the parliamentary system stabilizes, the actions of the Cabinet Minister are more and more dominated by his specialist, specific roles

rather than by his diffuse party roles. This is the reverse of the relationship between his overlapping roles in the early stages of a parliamentary system. The Cabinet Minister comes to identify himself with the civil service government bureaucracy, with whose senior members he shares attitudes and outlook as a result of similar educations, social backgrounds, technical skills, and responsibilities for effective government. The effect of this identification is to raise the status of the government bureaucracy.

2. As the party bureaucracy becomes stabilized, continues to recruit new party leaders, and gains experience, the persons filling specialist roles begin to acquire and exert greater authority; they move into roles which are more diffusely defined.

3. As the Cabinet Ministers on the front bench come to identify themselves more completely with the government bureaucracy, the party core, drawn primarily from the party bureaucracy, assumes increased control over the back bench of the parliamentary party because it is the party bureaucracy which enforces party discipline and selects party candidates for office.

4. The diffuse, all-purpose role, previously dominant over both bureaucracies, is less and less able to exert its dominance. In the Cabinet it takes on the characteristics of a specialist role, though still more diffusely defined than any of the roles subordinate to it in either the Cabinet or the government bureaucracy. Similar consequences occur in the political party aspects of the all-purpose role. As party leaders emerge in the party bureaucracy, the undivided support of the public for the all-purpose role is weakened, and it loses its symbolic status for the public, that group in the political system which initially sanctioned the all-purpose role.

If this conclusion is substantiated, certain consequences appear inevitable. The conflict between the party bureaucracy and the government bureaucracy, always implicit, becomes more open and intense. This is followed by a decline in responsible government, since each bureaucracy "tends to view the entire nation in its own image." Ghana appears, therefore, to be entering a phase marked by an interesting political dilemma, not unlike that of the French political system. In the absence of an effective opposition political party in the country, there is a strong possibility that the CPP will resolve this dilemma by itself becoming the government.

In the terms of this analysis, then, Ghana faces the problem of reducing a personalized, diffuse all-purpose role — in itself a potential threat to constitutional democracy — to a system of predominantly specific overlapping roles without precipitating a struggle in government even more threatening to constitutional democracy. Thus far Nkrumah and the various membership groups in Parliament have kept the conflict indirect and subtle without impairing the operations of government.

If Ghana can develop a responsible opposition, an alternative government in a real sense, committed to the constitutional order, capable of recruiting candidates for political office who possess a sense of party discipline and party organization, and capable of filling overlapping roles with qualified persons, the dilemma can be resolved in a satisfactory manner. Eisenstadt has pointed out that "insofar as other groups tend to participate more actively in political life, the monopoly of power and prestige breaks down, and the bureaucracy may thus become only one among a number of status groups, deriving many of its symbols from other groups and strata in the society. As the pressure from these groups becomes stronger, the bureaucracy tends to lose some of its autonomy." [7] The government bureaucracy becomes a neutralized, specific membership group in government, seeking the goal of effective government compatible with the basic, general rules of the society. The party bureaucracy becomes a neutralized, specific membership group in the political system but outside of direct intervention in government, because it must contend and compromise with strong opposition party bureaucracies for public support.

In this respect, the National Liberation Movement in Ghana has thus far been unable to provide the necessary kind of opposition, for the results of its efforts have been simply to strengthen the relationships between the party bureaucracy of the CPP and the Prime Minister and his Cabinet. The NLM cannot at the present time be regarded as a source of political pluralism.

Conclusion

The series of interim constitutions has been able to establish a functioning democratic system in Ghana. It is apparent that the system will be less stable than before, at least during the early stages of self-

[7] See S. N. Eisenstadt, "Political Power in Bureaucratic Societies," *World Politics*, Vol. IX, No. 1, October, 1956, p. 34.

government, for reasons discussed in this analysis. There is one other factor contributing to the instability of government in the near future, however, to which attention must be given. This factor is the omission from the pattern of constitutional development of any feature equivalent to the British Crown, that is, some symbol as meaningful to Ghana as "The Crown" has been to the British.[8]

Ultimately the concept of the state as a moral trust is essential to the functioning of a constitutional democracy, and it is solely to this aspect of "The Crown" that reference is here made (and not to such aspects as historical derivation from feudalism, the inheritance of office, the nobility, the class system, and all the other formal aspects of the concept). Perhaps the most crucial feature of the British constitutional system is the incorporation of this concept of moral trust into every role of the governmental system to a degree found in no other system. The concept of "The Crown" expresses the subordination and responsibility of each person filling a political role to that symbolic role. In a real sense, each role becomes a specific role; only "The Crown" is diffuse, all-purpose. This single role is the "property" of Her Majesty's Government. The sovereign is relatively powerless, but the symbol is powerful, and responsibility to it becomes peculiarly and personally the requirement of the occupant of every political role, including the sovereign himself. In the British pattern, there is almost a direct correlation between the rise in symbolic status of "The Crown" and the decline of personalized diffuse roles in the British Parliament. This is perhaps nowhere better brought out than in the position of Sir Winston Churchill, whose powerful personality was combined with an awesome respect for the limits and traditions of his office.

The interim constitutions in Ghana have created a set of political roles which interact and are integrated with each other. Roles have become increasingly specific and the degree of indeterminacy and freedom of action based upon personality or upon irresponsibility has been reduced. Up to the present time, however, the most crucial role in the government has not been sufficiently depersonalized. The Prime Minister still carries a "mystique" of public morality, not only in the eyes of his followers but also in his own eyes as well. He personally

[8] Constitutionally — unless Ghana should declare itself a republic — the Crown plays the same part in Ghana that it does in the United Kingdom.

is indeed the symbol of Ghana, of anti-imperialism, of self-government, of freedom, and in certain respects he regards the state of Ghana as his own creation and as an extension of his own personality and life.

"The Crown" cannot perform a function in Ghana similar to that which it performs in Great Britain or, to a lesser degree, in New Zealand, Australia, or Canada. It is to be hoped, however, that a functional equivalent will emerge which will supply that component essential to constitutional democracy, a sense of political propriety in the public and in those chosen for public office, a responsibility to the state itself as a moral trust. Perhaps this has been best stated by T. H. Green when he argues that the "real" function of government is "to maintain conditions of life in which morality shall be possible, and morality consisting in the disinterested performance of self-imposed duties."[9]

In the last analysis interim constitutions establish the bases from which further political development can take place. These bases have been well provided in Ghana. But interim constitutions are no guarantee of effective government. They can at best provide the mechanisms for resolving conflict. The public and those it chooses to represent it must decide if it wants those conflicts to be resolved.

[9] T. H. Green, *Principles of Political Obligation,* Longmans Green, London, Impression 1950, p. 40.

III

Local Politics and Democracy in Nigeria

L. GRAY COWAN, *Columbia University**

SINCE 1947 the government of Nigeria has been almost completely transformed. Federal and Regional legislatures have been created and within the past five years elected local councils have been substituted in Southern Nigeria for the former Native Authority system. For those interested in problems of political integration in a non-Western society, the changes at the local level have been of particular importance since it is here that the conflict between the new bodies and the indigenous political structure emerges most clearly.

For the vast majority of Nigerians the legislative assemblies at Lagos and in the Regional capitals have as yet very little real significance. The issues they discuss are too remote and too complex to be within the grasp of the illiterate peasant farmer. But since these legislatures have no counterpart in the indigenous institutions, the way is open for them to gain the undivided loyalty of the voters.

A more serious problem appears with the elected local council. It is a foreign political form which is being grafted on to an already operating political system to which the bulk of the people still owe allegiance. The values and standards represented by the two systems are often widely divergent, and the individual is required to choose between them. For most voters the political horizon ends at the village or district boundaries and the operation of the local council provides their only criterion for

*I wish to express my gratitude to the Rockefeller Foundation and Columbia University for financial assistance which made possible the field work for this paper.

judging the worth of the democratic forms. It has not been easy to introduce effective popular responsibility in the lower strata of the political structure and the process is still far from complete. In the following pages some of the problems of integration which have been encountered in the development of the conciliar structure will be briefly examined.

The Decline of the Native Authority System

It is impossible to discuss many of the present problems of local democracy in Nigeria without some reference to the Native Authority system that constituted the backbone of native administration from the inception of British control. Indirect Rule, as it was introduced into Northern Nigeria by Lord Lugard, was simultaneously an ideal and a practical administrative necessity. Faced with the problem of administering a territory of over 280,000 square miles with a handful of officers, Lugard had little choice but to make full use of the existing Emirate administrations. At the same time he was himself convinced that the most effective colonial rule was that which disturbed the indigenous social and political structure least. The Native Authority system which evolved out of this convenient combination of theory and circumstance was designed in the first instance to meet the needs of Northern Nigeria. In terms of its administrative usefulness it functioned relatively well and still does so today but basically it was, of course, an autocratic form. In theory it was presumed (albeit vaguely) that, over a long period of guidance by the British administrative officer, the native institutions would slowly evolve in a more democratic structure. But emphasis throughout the system was laid primarily on the development of modern administrative techniques rather than on popular representation.

Only after the amalgamation of Northern and Southern Nigeria in 1914, and the transfer of the Native Authority system to areas having a totally different structure of traditional rule did its defects begin to emerge. An inherent assumption of the Native Authority system was that all communities possessed certain natural leaders who wielded authority and who could command at least some degree of obedience from the people. Northern Nigeria, having been conquered a century earlier by the Fulani, corresponded in all respects to this preconception. The South, however, presented a more complex picture. Though the West had a well-organized hierarchy of chiefs, the locus of traditional authority was difficult to find in the Eastern Provinces and, even when it was discovered, it often proved of very little use for administrative purposes since the authority of the chief or clan head extended over too small an area.

The British administration assumed that the relationship between the paramount chief and the village chiefs in Southern Nigeria was similar to that between the Northern Emir and his District Heads. Consequently, it was expected that an order issued at the top of the hierarchy would be transmitted to the bottom and thus to the people. In fact the situation was often just the contrary. The village chiefs and the traditional councilors were under no compulsion to obey the orders of the paramount chief; rather he depended on them for his authority. He was the spokesman for his people but his word was far from law. In some tribes, such as the Yorubas, an accepted traditional method was available for eliminating an Oba who acted consistently against the advice of his council.

The Native Authority system could never be said to have been adapted in an entirely satisfactory manner to the structure of tribal institutions in the South. It worked with varying degrees of efficiency for more than thirty years, but even by 1939, it was evident that for a wide variety of reasons, its prestige was already declining. The increased pace of economic and social development during the war years only served to heighten the dissatisfaction with the system. It became one of the chief whipping-boys for the rising group of nationalist politicians in their struggle for self-government since it was so prominent a feature of British colonial control. The new political leaders saw the Native Authorities as a block to the progressive development of popular political responsibility in Nigeria. Certainly the Authorities were neither representative nor were they responsible to the popular will in the Western democratic sense. The chiefs and other traditional office holders from their side were disinclined to share the privileges and prestige of their position with elected members who, in their eyes, had no legitimate place in government. At the insistence of the educated minority several Native Authorities had a few elected members by 1950, but any expectation that they would voluntarily convert themselves into representative bodies was without foundation.

The unrepresentative character of the Native Authorities constituted a particular grievance for the substantial group in the Eastern and

Western Regions who had had the advantage of a British education, or who had benefited from the post-war economic prosperity to raise themselves well above the general living standard of their fellow citizens. For this group it was a source of growing irritation that they were allowed to play only a very minor, if any, role in local government. They felt understandably that the chiefs, who were often old, usually illiterate, and thus not competent to deal with complex modern administrative questions, should hand over to them the responsibility for tasks which they felt much more capable of performing. Perhaps more than anything else, it was this dissatisfaction with their role in the community under the Native Authority system in both the Eastern and Western Regions that prompted the African ministers to seek a new type of local administration when they finally rose to power in the Regional governments. Conversely, the lack of this educated element in the North in part accounts for the continuation there of the modified Native Authority system.

From another and more general point of view, the Native Authorities were rapidly becoming outmoded. The introduction of the elective principle for the legislatures in the Constitution of 1951 placed the Native Authorities in a somewhat absurd position. It was evident that Nigerians were considered capable of electing their own representative government on the national level but had not yet reached this point at the local level. The incongruity of a highly articulated democratic system at the top and largely unrepresentative organs at the bottom served only to strengthen the case of the political leaders who demanded sweeping changes on the lowest level.

The New Local Government Laws

It is perhaps not surprising that the first moves to replace the Native Authorities with elected councils came from the Eastern Region where the system was least well adapted to the indigenous political structure. After almost three years of investigation and discussion the Eastern Region Local Government Law was passed in 1950. The system of councils it established is based closely on the model of English local government. The councils are arranged in three tiers — county, district and local — and, with occasional exceptions, their membership is entirely elective. The local councils are directly elected; district and county council members are elected by the members of the local councils from among their own numbers. This indirect electoral system is slowly being replaced by a direct vote for the members of all councils but only with considerable difficulty. The parochial tendency of the voters to choose only a man of their own village poses serious problems in creating larger wards by combining several villages, as is necessary for direct election to the county council. It is difficult to convince the average villager that his interests are genuinely being represented by a man he does not know.

In general, the councils possess the normal powers to be found in English local bodies but because the urban areas are more advanced not all councils have the same powers. Each council, established by separate Instrument, has only those powers which it is felt the new body is capable of exercising. The system, therefore, has considerable flexibility; it is possible simply by amending the Instrument to place more power step-by-step in the councilors' hands as their experience grows. Control over the councils is exerted through the Regional Ministry of Internal Affairs, which is responsible for drafting the Instruments which set up the councils and for supervising all their activities. In their eagerness to make a clean break from the Native Authority system the drafters of the 1950 Ordinance virtually excluded the District Officer from any part in local government whatever. It rapidly became clear, however, that the councils would need more experienced guidance than had been at first assumed and, in 1955, a revised Law restored to the District Officer the power to attend council meetings and to report to the Minister any irregularities in the council's work.

Except for one or two important modifications, the Western Region Local Government Law of 1952 is almost a carbon copy of the Eastern Region legislation. A similar three-level council system is created, although, unlike the East, the top tier is termed the divisional, not the county, council. Perhaps the most significant difference between the two Regional laws lies in the larger place given to the traditional authorities on the councils. In recognition of the chiefs' control over larger territorial units, the Western Region Law requires that the membership of district and local councils be composed of both elected and traditional members. The Instrument establishing each council specifies the numbers of appointed traditional members and of elected members, although the Law requires only that in no case shall the number of traditional members be more than one-third that of the elected group.

The District Officer (or Local Government Inspector, as he is now known) attends all council meetings, and the councils must be prepared to accept any advice he may see fit to give.

The Northern Region Local Government Law of 1954 makes it clear that there is no intention of immediately substituting elected local councils for the present Native Authorities. The aim is rather to broaden the base of popular representation within the existing framework. Under the Law the position of "Sole Native Authority" is eliminated; all chiefs and Emirs must now be assisted by a council and in some cases they may no longer override the council's decision. If local district councils are given executive functions by the Native Authority they must have a majority of elected members and be assigned specific duties; otherwise they remain purely advisory as in the past. In addition a so-called "Outer Council," which has been in existence in many Emirates since 1948, is given legal recognition.

Prominent members of the community having no traditional posts may be appointed or elected to this council. But the formal principle of elective representation is by no means as far advanced as in the South and its development has been pushed at a very gradual pace. The Northern Region Ministry of Local Government argues that until the present level of literacy can be raised throughout the Region there is little point to placing more extensive responsibilities in the hands of councils that would be unable to handle them. In fact, it is claimed that even the present provisions for local representation go beyond public demand and much has yet to be done to make the average villager aware that he is expected to take an active part in demanding new local services.

It is beyond the scope of this paper to review the operation of the new councils as administrative bodies. Rather I should like to indicate some of the problems that have been met in Southern Nigeria in establishing the basis for local representation in a society which, though it is rapidly changing, is still, to a remarkable degree, tradition-oriented.

Local Democracy in Operation

Although the traditional systems of both Eastern and Western Nigeria contained elements of popular selection for certain traditional offices, it did not necessarily follow that the holders of these posts were responsible to the electors. Their actions were restricted not so much by popular will as by tradition, taboos, and magico-religious factors that were a part of the general beliefs of the tribe. It might in fact be said that in some cases the chief was more responsible to the dead, i.e., to the ancestral spirits, than he was to the living. So long as the chief and his councilors did not radically depart from traditional ways, the decisions on most day-to-day matters were left in their hands.

One of the greatest difficulties encountered in introducing the system of elected councils has been to establish the concept of civic responsibility in the minds of both the councilors and the voters. The Native Authorities were at least in some degree based on tradition, which lent their activities a certain respect in the eyes of the people. Until recently, authority for the average Nigerian in the bush has been represented by the village chief or by the administrative officer. Today, a new type of secular authority, the elected council, has appeared with powers previously held by both former sources of authority. But the new council lacks traditional sanction; it is composed of ordinary citizens whose mandate, unlike that of the District Officer, may be withdrawn at the next election. There is still a strong element of doubt and confusion in the voter's mind as to the legitimacy of this new organ.

If the voter is not yet certain of the new council's role, no more have the councilors found their place in the community. To many, especially the older group, much of the work of the council is a mystery; they are content to let the staff and the younger members discuss the more complicated issues. But membership on the council gives a certain prestige in the community and a power to grant favors which the new councilor never before possessed. Thus with his job as councilor goes also the opportunity to engage in the petty graft and corruption which is the bane of the whole council system, particularly in the East. All too often the councilor tends to see his council work not as a community service but as a means of increasing his personal income. The existence of graft in local government is, of course, in no sense peculiar to the Nigerian scene. But it is particularly dangerous there at this stage because tradition requires that family or clan interest be put before all other interests. The dilemma of the individual councilor is especially acute since, if he uses his position to secure special advantages for members of his family, he incurs the displeasure of the Ministry and risks losing his position; if he does not, he risks ostracism by his own family group.

The ambitious young educated man in a village may look on election to the local council not as a means of giving the village the benefit of his skills but as a means of acquiring ready cash to go into business. It will take some years of experience before the position of the councilor becomes regulated within the community. The essential question at the moment is: Can public faith in the new councils be created in view of the low standards of honesty which have been set by the younger councilors in the past five years? Even in those parts of Eastern Nigeria where councils have been operating since 1951 a villager will seek out the District Officer rather than his local councilor if he wants something done for him. In the first place he is not quite sure whether the councilor has the power to help him and beyond that he knows that he will probably have to pay for the councilor's help if he does get it. Until a sense of mutual trust can be established between the councilor and the voter the councils will never be fully integrated into the communities they are designed to serve.

Standing in the way of full acceptance of the secular authority of the councils is the continuing authority of tribal heads. The emphasis the political leaders of Southern Nigeria have placed on self-government and popular sovereignty in the past few years has tended to obscure the fact that the chief and his councilors are still very much a part of Nigerian life. Despite the inroads made on tribal authority by economic development, urbanization and education, there remains a substantial segment of the population for which the bonds of kinship and tribal affiliation are of vital importance. In bush areas the village chief and the clan head are figures of real influence; the uneducated man still looks to them for guidance. Even the educated young men, for all their criticism of the outmoded restrictions of tribal relationships, acknowledge that to gain popular respect in their communities they must first make their peace with the chief.

It follows, then, that the effectiveness of the conciliar system can in large part be measured by its ability to integrate into its operations the old elite of the traditional leaders and the new educated class. At the moment two lines of legitimate authority are competing on the local level for mass allegiance. The secular system will come out on top sooner or later but until the councils can command the loyalty now given to the chief, the situation in many communities will continue to be fluid enough to obscure the real foci of authority. The existence of this dual authority in the community makes the work of the local council much more difficult, particularly if there is antagonism between the traditional authority and some members of the council. In one local council meeting I attended, a letter was read from the head of a group of villages in the council area, complaining that even though he was the president of the council, he was never notified of its meetings. It appeared in the ensuing discussion that the failure to notify him arose from the conviction on the part of several members that he was deliberately sabotaging the council's activities by advising his people to ignore its orders. Not surprisingly, the councilors resented the chief's view that the elected body was merely a group of "small boys" playing at government without any real authority, and had simply excluded him from their deliberations.

Neither the councilors nor the traditional leaders have been able to determine their new roles since the locus of power itself remains undefined. The councilors are told that since they are the elected representatives the power to carry on local government is vested in their hands. But they are at the same time members of their village groups or clans and derive from this at least a residual loyalty to their chiefs. The latter, aware of the strength of popular devotion to traditional forms, see the elected councilors as the usurpers of a place that is not legitimately theirs. It cannot be overlooked, however, that, although the source of the council's authority lies in the Regional government (still a very nebulous body in the eyes of the peasant farmer), the council alone enjoys the power to tax — an important point when the community demands services that must be paid for from local taxes.

The result of this somewhat anomalous situation is often a temporary compromise which permits the council to get on with the job while leaving a part of the decision-making power in traditional hands. In more than one council I have seen the following procedure used. A question is discussed at some length and then postponed until the following meeting. At the next gathering the chairman announces that a decision has been made, the substance of which is accepted without further argument. Closer inquiry reveals that the problem has been resolved in discussion at the village or family level in consultation with the traditional authorities, and the announcement of the agreement in the formal council meeting is very largely pro-forma. Such methods tend, of course, to be more common in rural district councils where there are likely to be fewer educated members, but they are illustrative of the extra-conciliar role not infrequently played by the traditional leaders.

Traditional members are included in the elected councils of the Western Region through the provisions of the Law, but in the Eastern Region the more advanced nationalism and the more diffuse nature of traditional authority combine to provide a relatively small place for traditional office holders. No places are reserved for ex-officio traditional members except in a few communities such as Onitsha, where the Instrument establishing the Urban District Council specifically provides places for the Obi of Onitsha and for six members nominated from among their own numbers by the traditional war leaders, the Ndichie. In consequence, if the chief wishes to play a role in the council he must stand for election on the same basis as any other member of his village. Many chiefs are reluctant to do this, partly because they feel that it is beneath their dignity to engage in a competitive election and partly because in any case they do not agree with the idea of popular representation. Moreover, there have been occasional instances when an unpopular chief has been defeated with considerable loss of personal prestige — a situation which the chiefs are eager to avoid at any cost. There are several councils, of course, to which younger and more progressive chiefs have been elected who play a valuable role in lending traditional sanction to the council's decisions. Such a solution represents the ideal form of integration between traditional and secular elements. As time goes on this may become the normal procedure but thus far local government in the East has suffered from the virtual exclusion of traditional leaders.

The more successful experience of the Western Region in integrating the chiefs into the new organs of representative government has caused the Eastern Region leaders to take a second look at the role of the chief. A bill has been introduced recently into the Eastern Region legislature providing for the official recognition of certain categories of traditional authorities. It is not yet clear whether this is intended to be a prelude to appointing some of them to the local councils or even to the eventual creation of a House of Chiefs. In any event, it is evidence of a more realistic attitude on the part of the politicians to the facts of political life at the local level.

In the Western Region the position of the chief, particularly in Yoruba country, is much stronger. The traditional members appointed to all levels of councils are specified by their traditional titles. In the case of Ilaro District Council, for example, there are two traditional members to thirty-two elected members; in the Ibadan District Council, nineteen traditional members to seventy-three elected ones. While some of the older traditional members contribute little to the work of the council their very presence provides an element of continuity that serves to ease the conflicting personal loyalties of the voters. Moreover, since the traditional members are not required to resign prior to each election those who understand modern administration can improve the council's effectiveness by guiding the new councilors in their duties.

The integration of the chiefs into representative government at the local level will continue to be a most serious problem in Southern Nigeria for some years to come. It cannot be done overnight, nor can it be done entirely by legislation. It will have to come from a gradual welding of two loyalty systems: from an acceptance of the inevitable by the chief and a frank recognition by the elected councilors of the fact that without the backing of tradition they risk operating in a vacuum. The voters will give the new system their full faith only if they are satisfied that it incorporates those elements of traditional culture that are still important in their eyes.

The English local government system remained generally free of party politics until relatively recent years. Even though this is no longer true today there are many who still feel that there is no place for party issues in local councils, and who deplore the entry of factionalism into what should be purely local affairs. In this respect, however, Nigerian and British ideas fail to coincide. Owing partially to the peculiar circumstances of nationalist agitation under which the local government legislation of the Eastern and Western Regions came into being, party politics have tended increasingly to affect the council system. The parties have only gradually come to realize the importance of local councils as bulwarks of "grass roots" organization. Even now the use of party membership as a tool in winning local elections is by no means regularized. Party labels are used by candidates more as a convenience than from conviction. Thus the party tends to be employed as a vehicle for acquiring power, and membership in no sense represents a personal dedication to a political program. There is a tendency to switch parties after the election or to forget party affiliations entirely when they operate to a candidate's disadvantage. In one local election I witnessed in the Western Region the public statements of the candidates indicated they were divided about evenly between the two contending parties. One party came out well ahead in the election. By the time the first post-election meeting of the council was held, the former opposition candidates who had won seats firmly avowed either that they had been running as Independents or that they had now seen the light and were staunch supporters of the majority party.

Party commitment is, however, constantly tending to become more rigid. Urban voters are becoming more and more party-conscious as literacy grows; as the parties become better organized they will be able to exert more pressure on local adherents to hew to the party lines. Already in the large centers such as Ibadan, factionalism is presenting a threat to the efficient operation of the local government. Party strife in the Ibadan town council between the National Council of Nigeria and the Cameroons (NCNC) and the Action Group has been particularly bitter since 1954.[1] In a recent election the victorious party, on taking office, was accused, not without basis, of having turned out of their jobs all the supporters of the opposition on the council staff. The possibilities of political favors are becoming more apparent to local party leaders — and to the voters as well. In the Western Region, particularly where there is strong party competition, there is increasing emphasis upon village and district leaders as the nucleus of party strength. In the Eastern Region, the NCNC has a weaker opposition and hence there has been less pressure from above for local conformity, although it has not by any means been absent.

The opportunities offered by local political activity as a stepping-stone to higher office are just now becoming evident. The local councilor who is a strong defender of the party interests is drawing the attention of the party leaders. There is at least some evidence that county councils in the Eastern Region are being looked upon by the NCNC as a fertile source of new material for the party ranks in the Regional and national legislatures. While the possibility of higher political office may aid in attracting ambitious young educated candidates into local government work, it has the disadvantage of injecting a growing element of party factionalism into local councils.

---

[1] The NCNC, led by Dr. Nnamdi Azikiwe, is centered in the Eastern Region, while the Action Group led by Obafemi Awolowo, is largely a Western Region party.

Political parties play a role also in the conflict between traditional authority and the elected councils. At first the nationalists tended to ignore the traditional ruler as a holdover from colonialism but they have gradually begun to realize his value as an influence in local politics. Since the chief still retains a hold on the loyalties of the people he can be highly effective as a means of securing votes, and the parties are now beginning to make every effort to court his favor. In some rural areas the support of the chief can mean the "delivery" of a sizable segment of the popular vote; in many respects the chief becomes a useful tool in the hands of skillful party organizers. If the chief's support can be counted on, it becomes less important to spend time appealing to the individual voter; the chief, in other words, becomes part of a built-in local political machine. Realization of the peculiar role of the chief as a party adjunct has placed some politicians in an awkward predicament. They cannot completely deny past statements in which they have branded the traditional authority as a hindrance to progress. Yet they need his support and, as a result, they have taken an increasingly equivocal stand when discussing the chief's place in government. A final resolution of the parties' attitude concerning the chiefs depends on the extent to which the latter demand retention of privileges that the party leaders are not prepared to grant. As the elective system becomes more firmly accepted by the people, the chief's power to secure votes will diminish and the point may be reached when the party leaders will feel that the value of his assistance is no longer equal to the cost of maintaining him on a substantial salary.

The increase of political party influence in local government, particularly in the Eastern Region, has been facilitated by the wide powers of control over local authority granted the Regional Ministry of Internal Affairs by the local government legislation of 1955. It was felt in 1950 that, at least for a temporary period, the inexperience of the new councils would require the Regional government to exercise close supervision over their activities. The experience of five years served to reinforce this point of view and in 1955 the statutory control of the Ministry was made even broader. The present Law not only empowers the Minister to establish the Instrument specifying the composition and powers of each council but he may also order the dissolution of any council should irregularities in its finances or its operations be reported to him. He must approve appointments to the council staff, and the budget of every council requires Ministerial approbation. Recent revisions of the Regional system of taxation (Eastern Region Finance Law No. 1 of 1956) also tend to make local authorities more dependent on Regional grants by withdrawing sources of revenue previously open to them.

The conduct of many councils over the past five years may amply justify some tightening of the Regional government's control over them. But at the same time it can be cogently argued that the continued extension of such control may very well destroy the whole local government system which it is designed to preserve. Deprived of financial autonomy either in the collection or expenditure of revenue, local councils may very easily become mere appendages of the Regional administration. Moreover, the wide area of Ministerial power exposes the councils to the danger that they may be used as instruments to further the interest of the Minister's party. Council areas could be arranged to favor party strength, or individual councils might receive preferential treatment in the matter of powers or Regional loans if they happened to be strategically important from the party's point of view. Prior to the drafting of the 1950 Law in the Eastern Region it was suggested that the local council system should operate under an impartial Local Government Board but this was vetoed by the Eastern Region political leaders who considered local government too important a matter to be taken out of the hands of the cabinet.

The smooth working of the new elected councils requires much greater internal cohesion among tribal groups than now exists. Many Nigerians argue that the greatest stumbling block to the development of self-government lies in the persistence of ancient tribal animosities. In some sections of the Eastern Region it is only with the greatest reluctance that opposing tribes have been persuaded to send representatives to a single county council. A great deal of the bickering at such council meetings derives not from an honest difference of opinion on the issue under discussion but from the fact that a member of one tribe will refuse on principle to agree with any opinion expressed by a councilor of another tribe. The following incident illustrates the lengths to which such disagreements can go. The members of a District Council were invited by the Chairman of the County Council (which included members of a tribe to which they were traditionally opposed) to hear an address by a Federal Minister visiting the area. The invitation was rejected in a most peremptory fashion on the ground that if the Minister wished to speak to them he might attend their meeting but that they saw no reason to go to a meeting at which the members of the other group would be present. When one member suggested that the Minister might find it more convenient to speak to one County Council rather than to three District Councils he was hooted down. That the invitation had come from the opposition (the County Council Chairman) was regarded as sufficient evidence that the Minister was in collusion with their rivals and so the matter was dropped. While tribal animosities on this level are amusing rather than serious, they can create a situation in more important affairs in which they seriously impair the council's ability to operate.

At least one county in the Eastern Region which had been formed by forcibly combining three distinct groups has fallen apart as a result of tribal and linguistic differences. Officers supervising the new local authorities have suggested, in fact, that the county unit is by no means always suitable for Nigeria. While the larger county units may be preferable from the point of view of administrative efficiency and economy, they become unworkable if they do not correspond to the locally accepted ethnic divisions. One writer directly concerned with this problem points out that:

> "Differences of opinion between county councilors of different clan or district council areas have resulted in demands by dissatisfied groups for secession from the county and the formation of district councils outside any county organization. Minority groups have also expressed the fear that they would receive no share of the services operated by county council which is controlled by a large majority group. In other areas, again, mutual suspicions have prevented clans federating for county purposes although it has been quite clear that common services could be more suitably managed by a county council." [2]

The task of the elected councils in the rapidly growing urban centers of Southern Nigeria is made more complicated by tribal divisions. The influx of what one member of the Eastern Region legislature termed "foreign Africans" into the towns is resented by the old inhabitants

---

[2] E. C. Alderton, "Developments in Local Government in the Eastern Region of Nigeria," *Journal of African Administration,* Vol. VIII, No. 4, October 1956, pp. 169 ff.

who feel that the strangers are seizing land and commercial opportunities that do not belong to them. This resentment is doubled if the strangers belong to a tribe for which there exists a traditional dislike. The council is faced with the problem of satisfying the demands of all groups for the protection of their interests. If it takes measures to curb the stranger element, it is accused of prejudice; if it does not, it is charged with betraying the interests of the old residents. Here on a group basis is found the same dilemma as that faced by the individual councilor. Is his first duty to the town as a whole or to his own people? Although the average town dweller is considerably more sophisticated than his counterpart in the country, he is still not sufficiently cut off from the obligations of the tribal relationships to ignore them entirely. The majority of those who live in Nigerian cities maintain a close and active relationship with the country areas from which they came, as is evidenced by the many urban branches of Tribal Unions. Thus their thinking is still partially oriented in traditional patterns which are transferred to their social relations with other groups in the town. The same problems are to be found in different form in the towns of the Northern Region. There the traditional Northern dislike of Southerners is reflected in the existence of the Sabon Garis, the completely separate stranger suburbs, which are only very slightly integrated into the Native Authority of the Moslem city.

There is no easy solution to the difficulty of creating a true community out of the many small and often mutually antagonistic groups that make up the urban agglomerations in Nigeria today. Perhaps the best hope lies in the overriding influence of common economic interests that will eventually force the individual to place the good of the town as a whole before responsibility to tribe or clan. But until that point is reached the elected councilor will have to be a man of strong character to withstand the pressures that could easily make a mockery of the representative principle.

Conclusion

The present local councils in Southern Nigeria represent not a continuing development from the Native Authority system but a definite break from it. The cornerstone of Indirect Rule was the progressive adaptation of indigenous political institutions to meet the needs of modern government but within the framework of traditional authority. The elected councils are based on an entirely foreign model. Although concessions are made to the traditional office holders in the Western Region, they are no longer the fulcrum of local government.

Basically, the problems which have been outlined are transitional in nature. To create new political institutions by a stroke of the legislative pen is comparatively easy; much more complex is the process of giving them roots so that they will become organic parts of the society in which they are to function. The elected councils of Nigeria were never intended to be duplicates of their English counterparts. In the transfer from the English to the Nigerian environment modifications had to be made to suit the new setting in which the councils are required to operate. The system which will emerge after a number of years of trial and error will be an adaptation of the English form superimposed upon the Nigerian traditional political structures. It need not necessarily correspond to anything existing in England or America; the important point is that it provide the type of administration best suited to Nigerian needs. The councils fall far short at the present moment of modern standards of efficiency and public honesty. These defects can be corrected. The most serious hurdle to be surmounted is the lack of genuine public acceptance of the conciliar system. Nigerians tend to look at the new councils as creations of the Regional government, not as bodies over which they themselves have any real control. The councils can never become a permanent part of the community until they are able to come to terms with the chief and his council, whose cooperation is a prerequisite to full public recognition of the new organs.

From the viewpoint of the outsider, the break with the traditional system was perhaps too fast and too soon. Though tribal institutions can no longer undertake the tasks that have to be done, the chief will continue to be an influence in local affairs so long as the mass of the people still feel that he represents legitimate authority. Thus regardless of the position the system of popular representation assigns to him, his place will not lose its importance for some years to come.

On the other hand, it is obvious that local government could not continue to stagnate while popular representation was developing at the Regional and national levels. Political party organization could not stop short at the Regional capital nor could the voters who were given the opportunity of expressing their opinion on national issues be denied the right to manage their own village or county affairs. The integration of tribal authority and elected councils can be done only in small part by the Local Government Laws. It remains to the people themselves to devise the compromises necessary for the successful combination of traditional allegiance and popular responsibility.

IV

Emergent Federalism in Central Africa: Problems and Prospects*

Eugene P. Dvorin, *University of California, Los Angeles*

Two of the most vigorous and extended debates in the twentieth century on the advisability of a federal form of government have taken place in Africa. Faced in the first decade with the alternative of establishing a federal or a unitary form of government, the South African colonies of Natal, the Transvaal, Orange Free State, and Cape Colony ultimately agreed on a unitary government with a high degree of decentralization despite strong opposition, particularly from Natal. Today, nearly half a century after the formation of the Union of South Africa, federalism is still espoused in that province.[1] Still more heated was the controversy over the mid-century movement for closer association in Central Africa. To some people, the federation of the British Central African territories of Southern Rhodesia, Northern Rhodesia, and Nyasaland was a "deal in human souls" and "the biggest sale of Africans which has taken place since the slave trade."[2] To others, federation meant participation "in one of the greatest movements and in one of the greatest missions that any civilized part of the world has ever

*This paper is based upon the author's observations and research in Central Africa during 1955-56 under a grant from the Ford Foundation. Nothing herein should be construed as representing the views of the Ford Foundation.

[1]For a contemporary presentation of federalist sentiment in the Union see Dennis B. Craig, *Lost Opportunity. A History of the Federal Movement in South Africa* (Durban: Central News Agency, n. d.).

[2]Statement of Mr. John Dugdale, M.P., in *East Africa and Rhodesia,* February 5, 1953.

taken part in."[3] Not surprisingly, therefore, the Federation of Rhodesia and Nyasaland had neither an easy nor a happy birth. Yet its very existence is significant for its neighboring regions both to the north and to the south.

Already before the turn of the century, Cecil Rhodes, diamond magnate, member of the Cape Legislative Assembly, and, later, Prime Minister of Cape Colony, had envisaged a vast British federation or confederation extending from the Cape of Good Hope to the East African Highlands. This African empire, in Rhodes' view, would flank and rival in greatness the brightest jewel of the Imperial possessions — the empire of British India and the Indian States on the opposite side of the Indian Ocean. In his plans the Central African interior, known as "Zambezia," "Charterland," and finally as "Rhodesia," was merely an extension of a great united South African realm, a "United States of South Africa," which was to serve as the fundamental pivot from which the new empire would thrust beyond Lake Tanganyika. This dream of a pan-African federation, with a united Rhodesia-South Africa as its foundation, has never been absent from the political thought of South and Central Africa. The persistence of various proposals for a pan-African federation or confederation on the grandiose lines of Cecil Rhodes is an outstanding feature of recent African political history and provides the setting within which Central African federation should be considered.

In the July, 1910, issue of the *Journal of the African Society,* for example, an article, written by a Northern Rhodesian under the pseudonym "Africanus," put forward a scheme of confederation extending from the Sudan and Abyssinia to the Zambezi River. Under this plan Northern Rhodesia and Nyasaland would be linked to British East Africa.[4] In 1935, Dr. Godfrey M. Huggins, then Prime Minister of Southern Rhodesia (later, as Sir Godfrey, the first Prime Minister of the Federation of Rhodesia and Nyasaland), expressed himself certain that a "United States of Africa" would be formed of all the British territories from the Cape to East Africa. "I imagine," he said, "there will

[3]Statement of Sir Godfrey Huggins (later Lord Malvern) in *Rhodesia Herald,* April 3, 1956.

[4]Africanus, "A Central African Confederation," *Journal of the African Society,* XVII (July, 1918), pp. 276-306. The thesis is elaborated in "Further Thoughts on a Central African Confederation," *Journal of the African Society,* XIX (January, 1920), pp. 101-108.

be a separate union between the two Rhodesias and Nyasaland and between the East African territories. Then East Africa will unite with the Rhodesias and Nyasaland, and finally all with the Union of South Africa."[5] The Capricorn Africa Society, established in 1949, announced as its "greater aim" a proposed Central African federation to be linked in the future with an eventual federation of the British East African territories of Kenya, Uganda, and Tanganyika. At a later stage, it hoped that Belgian and Portuguese areas would also join in some form of closer association. In a map distributed by the Society, the territory of the scheme reaches from the Atlantic to the Indian Ocean and from the southern border of Ethiopia to the northern border of Natal in the Union of South Africa. Central African federation was regarded as the first requisite step, the germinating seed, leading ultimately to a complete revamping of a major portion of Africa as it exists at present.[6]

In 1952, at the time that details of the Central African federal scheme were being formulated, Roy Welensky (later Sir Roy and presently the Prime Minister of the Federation of Rhodesia and Nyasaland), along with Sir Godfrey Huggins and several leading members of the Kenya and Tanganyika Legislative Councils, signed a declaration of principles supporting federation of the Central African and East African territories.[7] In January, 1953, was formed the Federation League of Africa which advocated a federation comprising the territory of the Union of South Africa, South-West Africa, Basutoland, Swaziland, Bechuanaland, Southern Rhodesia, Northern Rhodesia, Kenya, Uganda, and Tanganyika.[8] The Union Federal Party, organized in South Africa in the same year, supports a "Federated States of Southern Africa." The masthead of its party newspaper, *Federal News,* includes a map revealing that the "Federated States" would include the Union, South-West Africa, Basutoland, Swaziland, Bechuanaland, Southern Rhodesia, Northern Rhodesia, and Nyasaland.

These examples serve to highlight the geographically strategic position of the two Rhodesias and Nyasaland. The new Central African Federation could serve as the *southern* limit of a federation or confederation extending northward, or the *northern* limit of a federation or con-

[5] *Rhodesia Herald,* April 25, 1935.
[6] *Greater Rhodesia The London Proposals Examined.* (Salisbury: Capricorn Africa Society, 1951), pp. 1, 7-8.
[7] *Times* (London), April 30, 1952.
[8] *Rhodesia Herald,* January 10, 1953.

federation extending southward or, alternatively, as the *center* of a pan-African federation or confederation extending from the Cape to Kenya. It should also be noted that Southern Rhodesia, Northern Rhodesia, and Nyasaland are situated at the geographical crossroads of African political advance within white settler communities. The Union of South Africa, particularly since 1948, has embarked systematically upon the path of *apartheid* — of which one facet is the maintenance of white political dominance. Not only is the South African Nationalist Government determined that the white man shall not abdicate his position of political and economic supremacy, but it also believes that the white community can ensure its survival in Africa only if it remains the sole master of its own destiny and that of the other races. In Kenya, in contrast, as the next paper makes clear, the African is already participating in the struggle for political power.

This contrast between the territories lying south and north of Central Africa gives particular significance to racial policy in the multi-racial state created by the new Federation in 1953. Even a cursory examination of the debates and literature of the federation movement from 1950 to 1953 makes it clear that the movement has been, in reality, a two-pronged affair: that along with the mechanics of federation went a distinctive philosophy of race relations. This new philosophy is still in its embryonic experimental stages,[9] but the essential features of "multi-racial partnership" are already apparent. In its simplest terms, multi-racial partnership is based on the conception of an eventual "balance of races" in determining public policy and the distribution of the fruits of economic endeavor. Whether such an experiment will succeed is problematical and its final results may not be known for many years or decades. But since 1950 the Central African region, heretofore politically inert, has been transformed into an area of political dynamism.

The translation of the paper provisions of a federal constitutional system into effective working relationships between the legislators, civil servants, and citizenry of the constituent territories and the new federal authority is a crucial period in the life of a newly emergent state. Under

[9]In 1952 the Northern Rhodesian Government published a draft statement on multi-racial partnership as a basis for local discussion. The full statement is presented in *East Africa and Rhodesia,* April 17, 1952. The doctrine is further elaborated in the so-called "Moffat Resolutions" moved in the Northern Rhodesia Legislative Council in 1954. See *Hansard* (Northern Rhodesia) No. 82e (July 29, 1954) cols. 616-668. A brief definition is contained in *Federal Party Policy* (Salisbury: Federal Party, 1953), p. 4.

any circumstances, federalism is a highly complicated form of government. When, in addition, as in Central Africa, the constitutional document is particularly complex and designed to maintain an extremely finely balanced mechanism of government, the problems involved in implementing it are compounded many times.

The student of government faces obvious problems in any attempt to observe the process of federalism in its earliest stages. The conflicts and tensions engendered between jurisdictions during the difficult transitional period tend to make him underestimate or minimize the areas of harmonious relationships. Moreover, some of the most useful tools available to the student of long-established federal systems cannot be used in examining emergent federalism. No one can foresee the role of the federal judiciary in determining whether federalism will be strong or weak, effective or unworkable, when the judiciary has yet to decide its first case involving an important point in constitutional law. Further, the period when Federal Ministers and civil servants are testing and probing with powers they have never exercised before and territorial Ministers and civil servants are adjusting themselves to diminished spheres of authority is hardly the most opportune time to gain an image of federalism other than in a state of extreme fluctuation.

This study, therefore, does not pretend to present either a comprehensive theory of Central African federalism or an all-embracing survey of governmental organization. Rather, it attempts to sketch briefly the nature and implications of certain selected problems of emergent federalism in the Central African Federation which comprises Southern Rhodesia, Northern Rhodesia, and Nyasaland. Four problems in particular are considered: (1) the division of powers; (2) the new Federal Civil Service; (3) the African Affairs Board and representation of African interests in the Federal Assembly; and (4) political parties and federalism.

The Division of Powers

A most useful characterization of the Central African federal scheme is a statement by the Prime Minister of Southern Rhodesia during the course of his testimony before a Commission of Inquiry. In speaking of Central African federalism, the Prime Minister described it as a federation "on the brink of amalgamation" so far as the distribution of governmental functions are concerned. "It was," he stated, "no ordinary

Federation we were given. It was as near a United Government as possible except that Native Affairs were kept out."[10]

The explanation of this curious hybrid lies in history. The British Government gained its powers of administration over Northern Rhodesia and Nyasaland through treaties of protection with the chiefs of Native tribes or through conquest. Imperial responsibilities for the protection and well-being of these indigenous peoples, it was felt by Imperial statesmen, could only be reconciled with European aspirations for closer association if the federal form of government included a division of powers which permitted continued British control of African affairs. Thus, African political advancement in Northern Rhodesia and Nyasaland, African local government, African land, and African labor remain territorial responsibilities. In these fields and in others not surrendered by the Colonial Office to the Federal Government, administration and government go on as before. The peculiar nature of the division of powers in the Central African Constitution[11] is, therefore, the consequence of the attempt to incorporate continued and unfettered British responsibilities in certain fields into a scheme which would also create a strong central government.

Other features of the Federal Constitution add further complexities. The presence of a lengthy concurrent jurisdiction list[12] tends to make the division of powers somewhat blurred and runs contrary to the original intent that the division of powers between central and territorial governments "should be as clear cut as possible."[13] (Under the latter theory no concurrent powers had been envisaged and the powers of government were to be either federal or territorial.) Moreover, though it is not common for federal constitutions to divide the *individual* and *specific* powers of government among the central and territorial authorities, the Central African Constitution provides that in addition to the concurrent powers the Federal Government shall have certain exclusive powers in respect to one territory while the other territories may exercise these same powers themselves.

[10]*Commission of Inquiry into the Siting of the Territorial Capital.* Typescript of testimony. (Salisbury: Southern Rhodesia Parliamentary Library, 1955), p. 19.

[11]*The Federation of Rhodesia and Nyasaland* (Constitution) *Order in Council, 1953.* Annex. *The Constitution of the Federation of Rhodesia and Nyasaland.* Hereinafter cited as *Federal Constitution.*

[12]*Federal Constitution,* Second Schedule, Part 11.

[13]*Central African Territories, Report of Conference on Closer Association.* Cmd. 8233, Ch. IV, para. 45.

One outstanding example of this unusual arrangement is in regard to non-African agriculture. In the Constitution, Southern Rhodesian non-African agriculture (including such subjects as animal husbandry, dairies and dairy farming, horticulture, agricultural colleges, and agricultural research) is on the Federal Government's exclusive legislation list. Non-African agriculture in Northern Rhodesia and Nyasaland is within the exclusive jurisdiction of the territorial governments unless the governments desire to have these subjects declared concurrent matters. The Northern Rhodesia Government took this latter action in 1955,[14] in order to place most aspects of its non-African agriculture under Federal control. This is the first major responsibility relinquished by a territorial government since federation was inaugurated in 1953 though the Northern Rhodesia Government still retains some functions related to non-African agriculture which the Federal Government has not taken over.[15] As a result, Northern Rhodesia non-African agriculture is now divided between two governments instead of being administered by one government as formerly. The Nyasaland Government, in contrast, has adamantly refused to transfer any portion of non-African agriculture to Federal control.[16] In all three territories African agriculture is exclusively a territorial responsibility and cannot be transferred to the concurrent list.

The subject of education is another unusual example of dividing the individual and specific powers of government. Education is divided in several ways: (1) primary education and secondary education of persons other than Africans, i.e., Europeans, Asians, and Coloreds, is an exclusive power of the Federal Government; (2) the primary and secondary education of Africans is not on the Federal exclusive or the concurrent jurisdiction lists and is, therefore, one of the residuary powers of the territorial governments; (3) higher education, *including the higher education of Africans,* is a power delegated exclusively to the Federal Government. Thus, in contrast to African agriculture which in all its phases remains a territorial responsibility, African education beyond the secondary school level is a federal responsibility.

---

[14]*The Non-African Agriculture (Transfer to Concurrent List) Ordinance, 1955.*

[15]The Federal Ministry of Agriculture in regard to non-African agriculture in Northern Rhodesia will take over the conservation and extension services which include animal husbandry, tobacco, crop and pasture advisory services, dairy and poultry farming, horticulture, and bee-keeping. The Northern Rhodesia Agriculture Department retains responsibility for forestry and irrigation. The production side of irrigation, however, comes under the Federal Ministry.

[16]See the statement of the Nyasaland Government in *Rhodesia Herald,* January 4, 1956.

The difficulty of attempting to divide education between territorial and federal authorities on the basis of its being African or non-African was illustrated by a recent public controversy. In March, 1956, the Southern Rhodesian Government announced a five-year plan costing £12,500,000 to make the African educational system more efficient, train more African teachers, increase educational facilities, and increase the number of African students completing secondary education.[17] Complaints soon followed from Europeans to the effect that the Southern Rhodesia Government was providing all this money for African education — but what were its plans for Europeans? Such complaints and questions were directed at the Southern Rhodesia Cabinet which originated and sponsored the new African education plan, and which became quite perturbed about the situation, and with good reason: for European education is a Federal and not a territorial responsibility. The Southern Rhodesian Government felt it was being unjustly criticized for merely doing its job and the Prime Minister finally made a public statement pointing out that since federation the functions remaining to the territorial governments were largely concerned with the African people, and that demands for more funds for European education should be directed to the Federal, not territorial, authorities.[18]

An unusual problem in the division of powers concerns the construction of one of the world's largest hydro-electric schemes at Kariba Gorge on the Zambezi River. This river is the boundary between Northern and Southern Rhodesia and, when completed, the dam will join both territories. In the early stages of construction, problems arose as to the regulations governing the employment of Native labor on the dam, since the provisions in the two territories differed widely. Not only would Africans from one territory working or injured on the opposite side of the river come under the regulations of the other territory, but such subjects as liability for injury, health and sanitation, housing standards, first aid, ration scales, labor records, rates of pay, overtime, machinery for settling disputes, and so forth, were involved. Moreover, while Northern Rhodesia had comprehensive provisions governing the employment of Africans throughout its territory which were therefore applicable to Kariba, regulations in Southern Rhodesia are laid down not on a territorial basis, but for specific industries. It is obvious that since the

[17]*Rhodesia Herald,* March 16, 1956.
[18]*Sunday Mail* (Salisbury), April 8, 1956.

Kariba project is under Federal jurisdiction[19] the simplest solution would have been for the Federal Government to formulate uniform regulations, but since African labor is a territorial subject the Federal Government was excluded from the field. One proposal was to declare the site an extra-territorial Federal area so that uniform Federal regulations could be laid down with a minimum of delay but this was abandoned as impracticable. Thus the Federal Government was left without jurisdiction over the regulations of African workers on a federal project. Only after several months of protracted discussions between the territories were the relevant laws on both sides of the Zambezi finally brought into line.

An extreme example of the consequences of the division of powers was provided by the fourth meeting of the Inter-African Labor Conference held at Beira in August, 1955. The membership of the Commission for Technical Co-operation in Africa South of Sahara, who sponsored the conference, comprises the governments of sub-Saharan Africa and the problems studied range over a large number of subjects one of the most important of which is Native labor. External affairs is, of course, a Federal function and an international meeting is within the exclusive jurisdiction of the Federal Government, but the subject of Native labor, the topic of this conference, is exclusively a territorial function. The Federal Government thus found itself in a unique and uncomfortable position: it was to be represented at the conference on a topic over which, as a government, it had no jurisdiction and since the subject was not within Federal powers it had no labor officer experienced in the technicalities of this field. The compromise worked out was that a Federal Government official was a member of the delegation as an observer but one of the territorial labor officers experienced in the subject was delegated to represent and speak for the Federal Government. The ultimate result was truly confusing, i.e., a territorial officer representing the Federal Government at an international meeting on a subject over which the Federal Government had no jurisdiction.

Attempts have been made to alleviate some of the unfortunate consequences of the existing division of powers. A Standing Committee on Labor has been established which is made up of two representatives of each territorial government with a Federal official as chairman. This

---

[19]*The Hydro-Electric Power Act, 1954,* empowers the Governor-General to create a hydro-electric project on any river in the Federation and empowers the Federal Minister of Commerce and Industry to set up a Board for construction of such a project.

committee is purely advisory but it meets frequently and discusses any topic concerned with the general problems of both European and African labor, thus providing some co-ordination in a field of obvious importance to all jurisdictions.

The problems involved in the division of powers also transcend the fundamental separation between matters African and non-African. Some aspects of social welfare, for example, are under exclusive Federal jurisdiction while others are either on the concurrent jurisdiction list, or, being unmentioned, remain exclusive territorial functions. The basis of most social work in Western society is the family unit. Yet, under the division of powers, it is possible for two governments to be dealing with the same family's social problems. School boarding grants are under exclusive Federal jurisdiction but because of its absence from the Federal or concurrent list, the relief of destitution is a territorial function. The close inter-relation between destitution and the granting of government funds to enable a child to continue in school is obvious, nevertheless policy remains the preserve of two separate governments. The "care and protection of minors" is a concurrent subject but in regard to neglected children, i.e., minors, there is almost always a considerable element of destitution — an exclusive territorial subject. In regard to some Federal subjects falling within the social welfare category, such as school boarding grants, medical aid grants, and old-age pensions, the territorial governments act as agents for the Federal Government. However, the territorial social welfare officers have little say in helping to form policy though the subjects they administer on behalf of the Federal Government may be inextricably intertwined with their own responsibilities.

The Federal Civil Service

Prior to Federation a commission was appointed to consider and report on the problems inherent in establishing a new Federal Civil Service. The report of the commission[20] sets forth the essential characteristics of the future service. Perhaps the most important principle it recommended was that the Federal Civil Service be primarily composed in its formative stages of territorial officers who voluntarily accepted Federal terms and

[20] *Southern Rhodesia, Northern Rhodesia and Nyasaland. Draft Federal Scheme. Report of the Civil Service Preparatory Commission.* Cmd. 8673 (London: H.M.S.O. October 1952).

conditions of employment. A second principle was that territorial officers who did not wish to make an early decision on transferring to the Federal service should, nevertheless, be allowed to gain experience in that service before they had to arrive at a decision. A five-year period of secondment from territorial to the Federal service was thus provided beginning from October 23, 1953, the date of the coming into force of the Federal Constitution. By the expiry of this five-year period seconded officers must decide whether they desire to accept permanent Federal appointment, revert back to the territorial service from whence they came, or request "abolition of office" and retire from public service altogether.[21]

Only those territorial civil servants who were in departments or portions of departments which were not brought under Federal jurisdiction had an option, however, on secondment to the Federal Civil Service. Those who were in departments or portions of departments transferred to Federal authority were compulsorily seconded to the Federal service to meet the need for experienced staff. But certain concessions were made to these seconded officers such as the assurance that they would not be transferred without their consent outside the territory in which they were serving. On October 23, 1955, two years after the Federation came into being, territorial officers on compulsory secondment were allowed to end their secondment or alternately to remain for another three years prior to making a final decision on whether to accept permanent Federal appointment, to revert to the territorial service, or to retire. Thus until the expiry of this three-year period in 1958, the Federal Civil Service is handicapped by a considerable degree of instability. Within the same department or portions of departments officers administering Federal powers may be either permanent Federal civil servants, seconded officers planning to revert to the territorial service, officers merely "filling out time" until they retire at the conclusion of the secondment period, or officers who are simply undecided as to their future. In addition, while on secondment to the Federal Government each civil servant continues to be the substantive holder of the territorial office in which he served immediately prior to his secondment and also to enjoy territorial, not Federal, conditions of service. Since

[21]Under the abolition-of-office terms the civil servant would be retired on a pension higher than the one he would have received had he resigned in the normal manner at the same stage in his civil service career.

territorial conditions of service vary widely, members of the same department may enjoy wholly different leave conditions and salary scales. Of still more importance is the fact that because of the wholly different background, experience, and outlook of seconded personnel, it is very difficult to develop an *esprit d'corps* in the Federal service.

At the root of this problem is a basic difference in the orientation of the territorial civil services, which results chiefly from the contrast between Southern Rhodesia's "settler service," based upon Central Africa, and the overseas orientation of many key civil servants in Northern Rhodesia and Nyasaland. It is true that about 50 per cent of the Southern Rhodesian staff is recruited from the United Kingdom, about the same percentage as in Northern Rhodesia, while Nyasaland is dependent upon the United Kingdom for the bulk of its staff. But the essential characteristic of the Southern Rhodesian service is that its members' permanent homes, interests, and life work are in Central Africa and that none of them is an officer in Her Majesty's Oversea Civil Service; in contrast, nearly 15 per cent of Northern Rhodesia's civil servants[22] and approximately 40 per cent of Nyasaland civil servants[23] are officers of Her Majesty's Oversea Civil Service (formerly "Her Majesty's Colonial Service").[24] Certain far-reaching results naturally follow. While Southern Rhodesian civil servants regard that territory as their permanent home a large proportion of the key civil servants in Northern Rhodesia and Nyasaland are directly appointed by the Secretary of State for the Colonies and their normal method of promotion is through transfer to other areas of the world. While some of these civil servants, whose children have grown up in Central Africa, have refused transfer, it is still the general rule that service in Central Africa is but one phase of their career. Thus it is not surprising that the former Federal Prime Minister, Lord Malvern, has already hinted that the Federal Government will eventually tend to abolish those portions of the civil services in Northern

[22]This figure furnished to the author by the Chief Establishment Officer of Northern Rhodesia. Letter dated March 19, 1956.

[23]This figure furnished to the author by the Acting Chief Secretary of Nyasaland. Letter dated February 25, 1956.

[24]Though the term "Her Majesty's Colonial Service" had been in use for over a century it was changed to "Her Majesty's Oversea Civil Service" in 1954. See *Colonial Office. Reorganization of the Colonial Service.* Colonial No. 306 (London: H.M.S.O., 1954).

Rhodesia and Nyasaland which are based upon Her Majesty's Oversea Civil Service.[25]

The new Federal Civil Service has followed the Southern Rhodesian pattern of demanding that its officers intend to reside permanently in Central Africa. Its terms and conditions of employment are designed to produce such a service.[26] The Colonial Secretary has given every encouragement to those of Her Majesty's Civil Servants seconded to the Federal Government to remain permanently in the Federal service,[27] and yet, as of April 1, 1956, only about ten per cent of the total number of civil servants from Northern Rhodesia and Nyasaland who were compulsorily seconded had accepted offers to join the Federal service. In the same period about two-thirds of the seconded civil servants from Southern Rhodesia accepted permanent appointments in the Federal service.[28] If these proportions do not alter considerably by the time the optional secondment period ends, the Federal service will be staffed almost entirely by Southern Rhodesians, while the Northern Territories will have an extremely low representation. This is the more likely

---

[25]"I am determined . . . that the public services of the three territories shall be based on Central Africa and the civil servants will be people whose homes are there, whose interests are there, whose life work is there and not, however estimable and fine a fellow he may be, a visitor from the United Kingdom who is only waiting to be promoted another step in another part of the world. These Colonial men have done grand work in these territories but the whole background is wrong for the purpose for which they are there, and *through federation we must hope to get that altered . . . It cannot happen all at once . . . but it should happen eventually.*" *Southern Rhodesia. Debates of the Legislative Assembly.* Vol. 33 (February 12, 1953), 4129. Italics supplied. Lord Malvern has suggested that all the public servants of the four governments of the Federation should be supplied through the device of a single public services commission. Until this came about there would never be that "loyalty to the Federation that was wanted. The Colonial Office is fighting it, but we will beat them one day." *Rhodesia Herald,* August 4, 1955.

[26]See: *Federation of Rhodesia and Nyasaland. Transfer to the Public Service.* P.S.C. 2'55 (June 1955). Issued by the Interim Federal Public Service Commission by direction of the Minister for the Public Service. *Federal Public Service (European Pensionable Branch) Regulations, 1955; Federal Public Service (European) Travelling and Subsistence Allowance Rules, 1955; Federal Public Service (European Pensionable Branch) Medical Benefits Rules, 1955; Federal Public Service (European Pensionable Branch) Grade and Salary Rules, 1955; Federal Public Service (European) Rent and Housing Allowances Rules, 1955; Federal Public Service (European Pensionable Branch) Conversion Rules, 1955.*

[27]"I hope that by the end of the five-year period the great majority of seconded Colonial Service officers will have transferred to the Federal Service." From the full text of the statement by the Secretary of State for the Colonies in *Northern Rhodesia European Civil Servants' Association Monthly Bulletin.* No. 41 (July 1954).

[28]Figures provided to the author by the Secretary of the Interim Federal Public Services Commission.

because out of the total of 4,979 officers seconded from the three territorial services, those from Southern Rhodesia totalled 4,090, that is about 80 per cent.

So far the Federal Government has taken over approximately 60 per cent of the existing territorial government services.[29] The Southern Rhodesian Civil Service had to supply the bulk of the Federal officers to carry out these responsibilities for several reasons: (1) The Northern services were small in number compared to Southern Rhodesia's 7,618 permanent officers just prior to Federation, not counting those engaged on contractual terms.[30] (2) As pointed out, a considerable percentage of higher ranking Northern officers were officers in Her Majesty's Oversea Civil Service and thus could hardly be counted upon to form the nucleus of the new Federal Civil Service which was to be wholly oriented to Central Africa. (3) As a seconded officer could not be transferred outside his own territory without his consent it was necessary that the Southern Rhodesian Civil Service supply the majority of Federal staff since the Federal capital is located in Southern Rhodesia. For this reason the Southern Rhodesian officer transferring to Federal service gains more and sacrifices less than his counterpart from Northern Rhodesia and Nyasaland.

An involved problem of selecting personnel for the Federal service arose in the early stages of transition to the Federal form of government. In territorial departments transferred *en bloc* to the Federal service there was no problem since the territorial services retained no remnants of those departments and therefore had no need of their specialized personnel. However, due to the division of powers, there were some cases in which only certain portions of departments were transferred to Federal control. Here a dilemma was faced in meeting the Federal requirements without damaging the remaining territorial element. Particular difficulty was encountered in the case of specific officers requested by the Federal Government for these officers usually held the higher administrative posts and satisfactory substitutes could not be easily or immediately obtained. Even though such officers might be anxious for secondment and eventual transfer to the Federal service, their release was refused if it was considered detrimental to the territorial service. It is still the case that if

[29]Statement of Sir Roy Welensky, Prime Minister of the Federation of Rhodesia and Nyasaland. *Rhodesia Herald* (February 13, 1956).

[30]*Southern Rhodesia. Annual Report of the Public Services Board for the Year ended 31st December 1954.* (Salisbury: Government Printer, 1955), p. 5.

territorial and Federal service needs conflict, the territorial authorities make the ultimate decision on whether territorial personnel shall be transferred.

This problem has yet another side to it which affects some of those officers compulsorily seconded to the Federal service who desire to revert to their territorial service. In the case of departments transferred *en bloc* to Federal authority, how can the seconded officer remain a substantive holder of a position in a department which no longer exists on the territorial level? In such cases, compulsory secondment has worked hardships on civil servants, for example, the postal employees. All postal and tele-communication functions on the territorial level were taken over by the Federal Government. From a practical standpoint, how can a postal officer with years of specialized postal experience revert to a territorial service which no longer has responsibility for work of this nature? How well can such a man fit into a continuing organization where he may be very "senior" in terms of postal experience but very "junior" in terms of the specific skills now required? Does he, in reality, stand a fair chance of promotion in a department where others have had continued service and have far greater proficiency in terms of departmental responsibilities? Thus, for a number of seconded civil servants the final decision must be made between accepting Federal appointment (with the possibility of compulsory transfer to one of the other territories) or retiring. For other civil servants such as law officers, for example, reversion to the territorial services presents no comparable problems.

The impact of federation upon the territorial services has not been uniform. Southern Rhodesia's service was decreased in size by 69.1 per cent.[31] On the other hand, because of the increased correspondence and need for consulting with Federal authorities, Northern Rhodesia's civil service has increased its personnel.[32]

In each of the three territories the inauguration of Federation led to the regrouping and reorganization of the administrative structure. Certain territorial departments were endowed with new responsibilities that they took over from other departments which had been relieved of some of their responsibilities through federation. Some territorial departments have undergone a complete reorientation as a result of federation, and

[31]Loc. cit.

[32]Statement of the Acting Chief Secretary of Northern Rhodesia. *Legislative Council Debates* (Northern Rhodesia). December 6, 1955, cols. 160-161.

there has been integration and centralization within the administrative structure as a whole.

One of the crucial long-range problems of the new Federal Civil Service concerns the role of the African in Federal employment. In both Northern Rhodesia and Nyasaland there are separate European and African Civil Services with differing conditions, yet together they comprise the total civil service complement. Both territorial services have been heavily "Africanized." Thus, in Northern Rhodesia, Africans in the Civil Service and police plus the African Teaching Service total about 14,000 persons in comparison to about 4,240 European civil servants.[33] In Nyasaland, African civil servants number 9,700 to only 850 European civil servants.[34] In Southern Rhodesia, in contrast, there are only 6,613 Africans in territorial employment[35] compared to about 5,770 European civil servants including those on secondment. Thus while Southern Rhodesia's European staff exceeds that of Northern Rhodesia and Nyasaland combined, the Africans in its territorial employment number only about one-half those of Northern Rhodesia and two-thirds those of Nyasaland. In addition, there are no Southern Rhodesian African "civil servants," as there are in the Northern Territories, since the Southern Rhodesia Public Services Act specifically excludes Africans from the Civil Service.[36] The Africans are thus termed "government employees."

Which path will the Federal Government choose to follow in regard to its own public servants? In this transitional period the Federal Government has been primarily concerned with determining the terms and conditions of the European civil servants and with problems of European secondment and recruitment. This has been necessarily so as the functioning of government itself depends upon European expertise and experience. Only after the European Civil Service has been adequately established on the Federal level and the period of secondment has ended, will the Federal authorities turn their attention to the problems of the

[33]This figure furnished to the author by the Chief Establishment Officer of Northern Rhodesia in an interview.

[34]This figure furnished to the author by the Acting Chief Secretary of Nyasaland. Letter dated February 25, 1956.

[35]*Southern Rhodesia. Estimates of Expenditure During the Year Ending 30th June 1956.* (Salisbury: Government Stationery Office, 1955), p. 3.

[36]"The service shall consist of all persons in the employment of the Government of the Colony and included in — (a) the administrative and clerical division; (b) the schools division; (c) the professional and technical division; (d) the general division; *but shall not include any native or coloured person.*" *Public Services Act,* Part II, sec. 8(1). Italics supplied.

African public servant. In this interim period Africans from the Northern territories on secondment to the Federal Government will remain, as the Europeans do, under territorial terms and conditions. A total of 2,345 African civil servants have been seconded to the Federal Government from Northern Rhodesia and Nyasaland. As there are no African civil servants as such in Southern Rhodesia, secondment to the Federal Civil Service is not possible. Southern Rhodesian Africans must therefore await the determination of terms and conditions for their *original* official entry into the Federal Civil Service. However, in the interim period, 6,450 Africans from Southern Rhodesia are serving as Federal "government employees."

It is doubtful if the Federal Civil Service will follow the Southern Rhodesian pattern in regard to Africans. The Preamble of the Federal Constitution refers to "partnership" between the races as a guiding principle of the new State. This principle is given form in a clause of the Constitution which provides that: "No person domiciled within the Federation who is a subject of Her Majesty or a person under Her Majesty's protection shall on ground of race only be ineligible for employment in the Federal public service, and in appointing or recommending any person for such employment regard shall be had only to his competence, experience and suitability."[37] Thus, Africans in Southern Rhodesia who are employed by the Federal Government will, in all probability, be integrated with those from the Northern territories into an African branch of the Federal Civil Service. Africans in Southern Rhodesian public employment, however, will remain "government employees" outside the territorial civil service.[38]

THE AFRICAN AFFAIRS BOARD AND REPRESENTATION OF AFRICAN INTERESTS IN THE ASSEMBLY

The presence and role of Africans in the Federal Assembly is probably one of the most discussed and debated subjects in the Federation's

[37]*Federal Constitution,* Ch. IV, para 40 (2).

[38]This divergence between Federal and Southern Rhodesian practice will merely be consistent with the present situation whereby Southern Rhodesia returns two Africans to the Federal Assembly but has traditionally not allotted seats for Africans in the Southern Rhodesia Legislative Assembly. The most authentic statements, parenthetically, have pointed to African membership in the territorial Assembly only in about twenty years' time. See *Central African Territories: Comparative Survey of Native Policy*. Cmd. 8235. (London: H.M.S.O., June 1951), p. 8.

African community. African representation in the Assembly is of particular importance as there are no Africans serving on Federal statutory boards or commissions[39] though Africans have sat on such bodies on the territorial level.[40] In the 35-seat Federal Assembly the so-called "African interests bloc" comprises nine members, three from each territory, six of whom are Africans.[41] Aside from their participation in the deliberations of the Assembly, the members for African interests have a unique role to play through the device of the African Affairs Board: a Standing Committee of the Assembly which comprises the three European members for African interests and one African member from each territory.[42]

The most important function of the African Affairs Board is to draw attention to any Bill or instrument having the force of law which the Board regards as a "differentiating measure." This term is defined in the Constitution as "a Bill or instrument by which Africans are subjected to or made liable to any conditions, restrictions or disabilities disadvantageous to them to which Europeans are not also made liable, or a Bill or instrument which will in its practical application have such an effect."[43] At any stage in the passage of a Bill through the Federal Assembly the Board may declare it to be a differentiating measure and lay a report to that effect, with their reasons, before the Assembly. If the Assembly passes this Bill the Board may request that it be reserved by the Governor-General for the "signification of Her Majesty's pleasure." When such a request is delivered the Governor-General cannot himself

[39]However, the *Federal Agricultural Marketing Act, 1955,* was so drafted as to allow for eventual African representation on the advisory Federal Agricultural Council. See the statement of the Federal Minister of Agriculture in *Rhodesia Herald,* March 14, 1956.

[40]In Northern Rhodesia Africans serve on the Advisory Board of African Agriculture. In Southern Rhodesia Africans serve on the Advisory Council on Education and the Land Board.

[41]The composition of the Federal Assembly may be briefly described as follows: Twenty-six members elected in the ordinary manner from single member constituencies of which Southern Rhodesia returns fourteen, Northern Rhodesia eight and Nyasaland four. In addition, each territory returns to the Assembly two African members for African interests and one European member for African interests. In Southern Rhodesia the two African members and the European member for African interests are elected from a common voters' roll. In Northern Rhodesia and Nyasaland the two Africans returned from each territory are elected by African councils while the single European member for African interests from each territory is appointed by the Governor.

[42]The three African members of the Board are selected by majority vote of the European and African members for African interests. The Chairman is chosen from among members of the Board by the Governor-General.

[43]*Federal Constitution,* Ch. VI, para. 71 (2).

assent to the Bill, except under special conditions,[44] but must reserve it for the "signification of Her Majesty's pleasure" and send the Board's request, together with the Bill, to the Secretary of State. This function of the African Affairs Board points up one of the most fundamental principles of the Central African federal system: namely, that even within its so-called "exclusive sphere" the Federal Government is not omnipotent. While it possesses independent powers of legislation, its powers of implementation may be curbed.

The African Affairs Board has been subjected to intense criticism by those who see little tangible evidence of its ever being anything more than a "stooge" device. Many people who felt that the Federal Government's Defense Bill and Cadet Corps Bill discriminated against Africans as a race were disturbed by the fact that the Board had not deemed such legislation discriminatory. In the former measure, Africans were excluded from compulsory peace-time military training while other races were subject to the provisions of the Bill. In the latter one, there was no provision for establishing Cadet Corps units at African schools though the Bill provided for compulsory military training in the Corps for all male students in European schools. The Board's failure to act in these cases seemed to suggest that it was ineffectual. It is interesting to note, however, that the Africans in the Assembly did not present a united front on these allegedly discriminatory provisions. Thus, any attempt by the African Affairs Board to have this legislation reserved might well have been handicapped from the start. Moreover, later events tend to support the thesis that the Board was waiting for a major issue before taking any formal action since the latter might have profound repercussions both in Central Africa and the United Kingdom.

When, in 1957, the Federal Assembly approved with a two-thirds majority the Constitution Amendment Bill to increase the membership of the Assembly from thirty-five to fifty-nine, keeping the same ratio as before so that only six of the additional twenty-four members had to be African, the African Affairs Board formally requested that the Bill be reserved on the grounds that it was a differentiating measure. As in the

[44]If he satisfies himself that it is not a differentiating measure and that the reasons given by the Board are "of an irrelevant or frivolous nature" or "if he is satisfied upon representations by the Prime Minister that it is essential in the public interest that the Bill be brought into immediate operation." If the Governor-General does so assent, however, the Bill must be forwarded to the Secretary of State together with the Board's request and a statement of his reasons for assenting. *Federal Constitution,* Ch. VI, para. 75 [4 (a) (b)].

earlier cases, Africans in the Assembly did not present a unanimous front against the measure. Yet the Board's decision to oppose the Bill shows its realization that it had far-reaching implications for the racial balance of power in the Assembly. This is the more so because the measure opens the way for the Federal Government's proposed two-tier franchise legislation to establish both a General Voters' Roll for those with an income of at least £300 a year and a Special Voters' Roll for those below that level. This division, in practice, will mean that almost all Africans will be on the second roll which will select relatively few representatives, while, still more disturbing to African nationalists, at least half the African representatives for the new Assembly will be chosen by a predominantly European voters' roll.

Despite the action taken by the African Affairs Board, the Constitution Amendment Bill was approved by the Conservative majority in the British House of Commons. The ultimate effect of this development cannot fully be foreseen. One immediate consequence may be a further loss of African confidence in the United Kingdom as a "protecting power." In addition, there may be increased pressure to abolish the African Affairs Board,[45] not only by those who have consistently regarded it as an exotic element foisted upon the Federal Government, but also by those who feel that whatever arguments the Board may make regarding legislation can have little effect within the inherently "political" environment in which the United Kingdom Government would have to make its decision. This latter view anticipates that a refusal of the Royal Assent to legislation which the Federal Government is determined to put into effect would result in a general election in Central Africa to secure a direct mandate on that particular issue. Such a development would subject the relationship between the Federation and the United Kingdom to the kind of controversy and re-evaluation which both are determined to avoid. Thus it seems inevitable that the Board can never hope to attain the potential which its foremost advocates originally envisaged.

Noteworthy is the fact that the Federal Government engages in frequent consultation with the United Kingdom Government on proposed legislation but has always refused to consult with the African Affairs Board. This fact suggests that the decision of the United Kingdom

[45]The most opportune time to press this position will be during the required review of the Constitutional document between 1960 and 1962. *Federal Constitution,* Ch. VIII, para. 99.

Government to advise or withhold the Royal Assent may well be known to the Federal Government even while legislation is in its most embryonic stages. If this is the case it is evident that the formal powers of the African Affairs Board are largely illusory and also that they can have little effect even as a psychological deterrent. To what extent Her Majesty's Government itself tries to prevent the Federal Government from embarking upon legislation which is blatantly discriminatory is not yet known.

The roles of the African and European representatives for African interests in the Federal Assembly also deserve some attention. It is incorrect to assume that these roles coincide. Usually they do not, especially as regards the European representatives and the African representatives from Northern Rhodesia and Nyasaland. The European representative for African interests tends to vote solely in the light of what he conceives to be the interests of Africans regardless of African views. On the other hand, the African representatives for African interests from the Northern Territories almost always vote in response to African opinion, which is important since it is the only means by which such African opinion can be laid before the Federal Assembly.

In addition, there is an important split between the African members of the Federal Assembly from Southern Rhodesia and those from Northern Rhodesia and Nyasaland due, to a considerable degree, to their respective electoral systems. In Southern Rhodesia the two Africans are elected upon the common voters' roll, which is essentially a European voters' roll since it contains fewer than 450 Africans. As a consequence, the Africans returned to the Assembly from Southern Rhodesia are moderates who are amenable to the European voters. But in Northern Rhodesia and Nyasaland, Africans are returned to the Assembly from wholly African councils and are more radical in their views as they do not need European votes either to gain or to retain their seats. There are indications that the African representatives from Southern Rhodesia are becoming increasingly divorced from prevalent African opinion, a fact that makes less significant the tendency of Southern Rhodesia's African representatives in the Assembly to vote the same way as the European representatives.

This experience reinforces African objections to the new franchise provisions sponsored by the Federal Government. Not only will Europeans throughout the Federation have an important and perhaps dominant share in selecting the African members of the Assembly but the Assembly seats specifically set aside for African members representing African interests will disappear in favor of the Government-sponsored "non-racial" approach to public policy. Europeans in the Assembly may no longer, therefore, have to listen to "radical" African views, but the price can be very high. If African sentiment, regardless of how distasteful it may be to European ears, is not *accurately mirrored* in the Assembly it may well seek outlets for expression in extra-parliamentary channels.

Political Parties and Federalism

In any evaluation of Central African federalism the policies of the political parties must be considered. As early as 1912 Europeans were forming political parties based largely upon differences in constitutional matters, i.e., advocating the termination of British South Africa Company administration, agitating for various forms of self-government or for amalgamation with the Union of South Africa. The indigenous population had not reached the stage where it had developed a political consciousness, nor indeed a political importance. Today it is difficult to imagine political campaigning divorced from racial issues. The problems of federalism and race relations are hardly separable for the future of federation, both its structure and its viability, is decisively linked to the resolution of political issues which are dominated by racial considerations.

The dominant political party in the Federation has been the Federal Party,[46] now renamed the United Federal Party since its fusion with the United Rhodesian Party of Southern Rhodesia in November, 1957. The United Federal Party which forms the present Government with twenty-four of the thirty-five seats in the Assembly, advocates the political doctrine of partnership. Throughout its four years of office it has studiously avoided any precise definition of the essential principles of partnership, preferring that these develop out of experience and circum-

[46]In December, 1953, Central Africa held its first Federal election to return members to the Federal Assembly. The Federal Party gained an overwhelming victory in terms of seats. Of the twenty-six seats filled by election in the ordinary manner the Federal Party gained twenty-four. The two African representatives for African interests from Southern Rhodesia were members of the Federal Party and had been endorsed by that party; with their election to the Assembly a total of twenty-six members in the Assembly were "Federals." The Federal Party lost two of these twenty-six seats in subsequent by-elections.

stances. Rejecting rigid definitions of racial policy and emphasizing gradualism in African social and political advancement, the Federal Party stresses economic answers to racial problems, and uses economic arguments in setting forth the advantages of Federation to Africans. Subscribing as it does to the doctrine of "equal rights for all civilized men," the party has proposed the limited development of a common voters' roll for Federal elections, but with techniques that will ensure and maintain European control of legislative and executive power. Thus, African advance is to take place within a framework in which Europeans remain the undisputed senior members of any racial partnership in the foreseeable future.

Of the two main opposition parties in the Federal Assembly, one is identified with European, the other with African interests. Both are critical and suspicious of multi-racial partnership and both are associated with groups which oppose or have opposed the present form of federalism. Today the principal European opposition in the Federal Assembly is the Dominion Party. It consists of groups of opposition elements which have differing and conflicting interests, but are united in their repudiation of the principle of partnership defined in terms of evolving social and political institutions which are common to both Europeans and Africans.

Prior to its disappearance from the political scene in late 1955, the Confederate Party was the first rallying point of these opposition elements. Though the Confederate Party gained only one seat in the Assembly, in the first Federal elections in 1953, it polled nearly thirty per cent of the total vote. Its policy of racial-geographical separation or "partition," as it is termed in Central Africa, has had, therefore, a not inconsiderable following among the European electorate. The Confederate program revolved around the conception of creating separate white and black states — the latter being generally referred to as "Bantustans" — and approximated in its essential details and terminology the theory of ideal, or total *apartheid* in the Union of South Africa.[47] The Confederates had no consistent ideas about whether the Native States would always be subject to Federal jurisdiction or whether, as they approached self-government, they would come under United Kingdom administration. Yet one principle was generally adhered to: the

[47]For further details see Eugene P. Dvorin, *The Central African Federation: A Political Analysis*. Unpublished Ph.D. dissertation, University of California, Los Angeles, 1955, pp. 380-99.

Bantustans were not to become independent African States but always to remain integral parts of Federal territory.[48]

As the Confederate Party passed into history, due to the appointment of its Party leader to the Southern Rhodesia judiciary, another supporter of partition, the Commonwealth Party, soon arose as a splinter group, which attempted to mobilize the opposition. The Commonwealth Party policies represented a more highly developed, more consistent, and more extreme form of partition than did Confederate policy. In essence, the Commonwealth Party proposed the amalgamation of Southern Rhodesia with the areas of heaviest European settlement in Northern Rhodesia — the line of rail leading from the south to the Northern Rhodesian Copperbelt and the Copperbelt itself. This plan would split Northern Rhodesia into three parts, i.e., North-Eastern Rhodesia, the Central-railroad-Copperbelt portion amalgamated with Southern Rhodesia, and North-Western Rhodesia. Under the Commonwealth Party plan, North-Eastern Rhodesia and Nyasaland (to be named "Eastern Protectorate") and North-Western Rhodesia (to be named "Western Protectorate") would become Native Protectorates or States under the joint trusteeship of the Federal and United Kingdom Governments. This arrangement would be merely transitory, however, for in time the Native States would secure full self-government and be allowed to secede from the Federation and to sever any formal administrative links with the European area and the United Kingdom Government.[49] The remaining European portions of Central Africa, thus relieved of their former areas of heaviest African concentration, would then be able to enjoy unitary government without the disadvantages of the present constitutional division of powers. Full and independent membership in the Commonwealth would follow as a matter of course.[50]

Though it gained one seat in the Federal Assembly in a by-election late in 1955, the Commonwealth Party never succeeded in attracting the other splinter opposition groups to its leadership or policies. It was

[48]See: *Details Given of Confederate Native Policy* (Salisbury: The Confederate Party, 1953); *The Confederate Statement of Principles* (Salisbury: Secretary, The Confederate Party, 1953); *Rhodesia Herald,* January 25, 1953. It was only during the last few months of the Confederate Party's existence that the Party leader mentioned the possibility of African areas eventually breaking away from the Federation. See the statement of Mr. J. R. Dendy Young in *The Chronicle* (Bulawayo) November 3, 1955.

[49]Author's interview with Mr. G. F. M. van Eeden, Leader of the Commonwealth Party.

[50]The broad outlines of the Commonwealth Party program are set forth in G. F. M. van Eeden, *The Road to Sanity* (Lusaka: G. F. M. van Eeden, 1955).

dissolved within a year and its leaders joined the Dominion Party which now includes the majority of all opposition elements. As a result of victories in two significant Federal by-elections, the Dominion Party, though it has been in existence for only two years, has emerged as a united and stable opposition capable of challenging the parliamentary dominance of the Federal Party. Though it supports the territorial integrity of the Federation, and has skillfully avoided doctrinaire policies of "partition," the party is nonetheless wedded to policies of "separate" development. In its view, political power must be retained by Europeans for generations to come, and the future development of the Federation is primarily the trust and responsibility of Europeans and not of an evolving partnership with Africans. The leader of the Dominion Party, Mr. Winston Field, believes his party's approach to African advancement may be compared to the paternalism of Belgian Congo administration, where economic well-being is stressed rather than political education and participation. In proposing that the way to racial harmony lies in giving each racial group the opportunity to develop its political capabilities in its own sphere under overall European control, the Dominion Party is bidding for power with what is, in fact, a doctrine of *apartheid*. If it secures office, the Party intends to abolish the Federal Party's type of franchise to ensure continued white dominance by restricting African participation on a common voters' roll. Basic to Dominion Party policy is a severe limitation of African political influence until the economic development of the Federation has resolved the unfavorable racial balance by attracting large-scale immigration.

The African opposition in the Federal Assembly is based on the African Congresses of Northern Rhodesia and Nyasaland who are represented for all practical purposes by the four African M.P.'s from these territories. The Congresses, which possess most of the characteristics of full-fledged political parties, are highly suspicious of multi-racial partnership and have consistently opposed federation between the two Northern Territories and Southern Rhodesia. Today, four years after the inauguration of Federation, they vigorously espouse the withdrawal of Northern Rhodesia and Nyasaland from the Federal State.[51] The Nyasaland Congress

[51]Not only have the four of the six African Federal M.P.s been Congress members but on the territorial level three of the four African members in the Northern Rhodesia Legislative Council belong to Congress, and in Nyasaland's first territorial election, held in March, 1956, active Congress members and Congress supporters were returned to all of the five African seats in the Legislative Council. The African Representative Council

has been most sympathetic to the Commonwealth Party's partition plan because Nyasaland would not only retain its present territory intact, but might realize the Congress goal of an African self-governing State. The Northern Rhodesia Congress is in a more difficult position. While it likewise supports the objective of African self-government, its members oppose any partition program which would divide Northern Rhodesia Africans into two States separated from each other by the intervening European area of the Copperbelt and the line of rail. In addition, the European area would comprise the wealthiest and most productive portion of Northern Rhodesia.[52] The important point, however, is that both Congresses agree on the principle that the Federation must be broken up.[53] The Nyasaland Congress even expelled the Nyasaland African M.P.s from its ranks late in 1957 on the grounds that their presence in the Federal Assembly gives the erroneous impression that Africans support and condone the Federation.[54]

Mention should also be made of the recently formed Constitutional Party which includes among its founders Dr. Alexander Scott, the Independent Federal M.P. from Lusaka. The Constitutional Party has rooted its political philosophy in the fundamental principles of the Capricorn Africa Society. It seeks to establish a society in Central Africa free from racial discrimination; it opposes granting Dominion status to the Federation or any further constitutional changes until its political principles are incorporated within the Federal Constitution. Though it rejects the concept of universal adult franchise, the Party accepts the principle of a

---

of Northern Rhodesia and the African Protectorate Council of Nyasaland, the highest African advisory bodies in those territories, have predominant Congress membership. In Northern Rhodesia the figure is approximately three-quarters and in Nyasaland virtually all Council members belong to Congress. The actual strength of the Congresses and the degree to which they are representative of African opinion are controversial questions. In terms of paid membership and active participation in Congress activities the numbers are probably only a few thousand in each territory. But if one considers how many Africans are wholly sympathetic to Congress programs and objectives, then the Congresses appear to be representative of a very large segment of African opinion.

[52]*Press Communique on the van Eeden Partition Plan* (Lusaka: Northern Rhodesia African National Congress, December 25, 1954).

[53]See *Report of the Deliberations of the 11th Annual Conference of the Nyasaland African Congress held at Lilongwe, Nyasaland, from 8th to 11th April, 1955.* (Nyasaland African Congress), pp. 1-2; *Statement and Message to the People of the Protectorate of Northern Rhodesia by the President General given at Chibolya of the 6th March, 1955.* (Lusaka: Northern Rhodesia African National Congress), p. 2.

[54]*Congress Views on the Extraction of Nyasaland from the Federal Scheme and the Representation of Nyasaland Africans in the Federal Assembly.* (Zomba: Nyasaland African Congress, September 25, 1955), Appendix, p. 3.

common voters' roll with qualifications less restrictive than those of the Federal Party. It differs fundamentally from the Federal Party in the stress it places on achieving an integrated society and establishing a political framework for the common development of Europeans and Africans.

Dissatisfaction with, and desire to abolish, the federal form of government in Central Africa is not restricted to the European and African opposition elements which have been described. There are also persons who tend to regard federation as only an interim consolidating device which should eventually culminate in unitary government. This position is based upon the thesis that it is virtually impossible to attain any degree of efficient government under the present division of powers and, moreover, that the European population of Central Africa, comprising 270,000 persons (as of June 30, 1957), the size of a British electoral constituency, is unable in terms of talent and finances to support four legislatures, four public services, four judicial systems, three governors and a Governor-General. Expressive of this school of thought is the Economic Party, formed in early 1956, which advocates a unitary state with one representative of the Crown and one House of Representatives.[55] In addition, a symposium of the views of members of the four legislatures on the subject of unitary government has been published and widely circulated.[56] One of the most frequently heard arguments in favor of retaining Salisbury as the site of the territorial as well as Federal capital was the assertion that unitary government would come about eventually and it was therefore wiser to leave things as they were.

Conclusion

In conclusion, what can one say about the prospects for Central African federalism? From the standpoint of administration there is little doubt that matters would have moved more smoothly if planning in terms of administrative feasibility had taken place prior to the political union of the three territories. The future compulsory review of the Constitution will, in all probability, not result in its drastic revision. The particular division of powers at the root of many of the day-to-day problems of

[55]See the advertisement of the Economic Party in *Rhodesia Herald,* March 2, 1956; also the statement of Mr. G. J. Taylor, founder of the Party, in *Rhodesia Herald,* January 18, 1956.

[56]"A Symposium: Members of Four Parliaments Express Views on Unitary Government" in *The Next Step: Federation's Future,* Sydney H. Veats, ed. (Salisbury: The Rhodesian Graphic, 1955), pp. 66-75.

administration may be subjected to minor adjustments. Yet, it is a moot question as to just how effective minor adjustments can be.

The uncertainties of the present period of optional secondment in the Federal Civil Service, reinforced by difficulties in administering the Constitution, have produced a feeling of discontent and uneasiness among Federal public servants. In long-range perspective perhaps the most important underlying factor is the difficulty of civil servants acquiring a deep-rooted sense of loyalty to the Federation they are committed to administer when such loyalty is absent from significant and vocal segments of the body politic itself. This is one facet of the problem of the "public spirit" of this new state — a problem outside the efficacy of Constitutional clauses and provisions.

Ultimate success of the Federation does not depend upon the solution of administrative problems. One must look beyond the "mechanical" aspects of government to the behavior and attitudes of the human beings concerned, and in particular to the contacts between the races. The issues involved become especially acute in the distribution of political power and the fears and suspicions of Africans toward the Federation will, in all probability, be reinforced by the recent franchise proposals of the Federal Government.

Differences in party views on the ideal state of the future reflects serious cleavages in Central African political thought. The implications for Central Africa's future are serious if these ideologies should be relentlessly implemented by alternating governments. It is of the utmost importance, therefore, that the direction of racial policy be decided soon and for all time.

There have been achievements as well as problems in this exceedingly difficult transitional period in the Federation of Rhodesia and Nyasaland. Many of these achievements are obscured from view unless the observer takes special pains to scratch and ferret beneath the surface during the process of consolidation. The Federal Government has not only produced a mass of essential legislation to enable it to undertake its responsibilities, but has embarked upon a bold and imaginative program for economic development and utilization of the nation's natural resources. It has well demonstrated the acknowledged British genius for innovation and adaptability in the field of government. That there are large numbers of persons determined to make federation work cannot be denied. On the other hand, the Federal edifice may, in reality, be built upon a fractured foundation.

V

Political Conflict and Change in Kenya*

CARL G. ROSBERG, JR., *African Studies Program, Boston University*

THE Colony and Protectorate of Kenya[1] in the post-war period has been the scene of political and social conflict of which the Mau Mau rebellion was only the most widely known manifestation. The Mau Mau rebellion was contained and defeated by a combination of police and military action, but the larger process of rapid social change continues. Indeed, this process is accelerating. Further, it is providing Africans with greater social and spatial mobility than has hitherto existed. Although it is not comparable in degree and extent with that in West Africa, the process of change in Kenya can be observed politically in the emergence of new African leaders and associations, trade union activities, increased political awareness, and demands for major constitutional revision.

The distinctive characteristic of present-day Kenya, however, is not merely the rapidity of social change, but rather the abrupt manner in which this change is affecting power relationships. The demands and

* The author wishes to acknowledge his appreciation to the Ford Foundation and the African Research and Studies Program of Boston University for research grants which have enabled him to study political problems in Kenya. The opinions and conclusions are those of the author and are not necessarily those of either the Ford Foundation or the African Research and Studies Program.

[1] On July 23, 1920, with the publication of the Kenya (Annexation) Order in Council 1920, the territories formerly included in the East Africa Protectorate were annexed to the British Crown and became the Colony of Kenya, with the exception of a ten-mile strip of coastline which remained part of the Dominion of His Highness the Sultan of Zanzibar. The latter territory was called the Protectorate of Kenya. For all practical purposes the Colony and Protectorate of Kenya are governed as one.

expectations generated by change and conflict are creating critical problems in adjustment and accommodation. To provide for stability and order requires a new basis of consent which, in turn, will be dependent on the power relationships evolving in the territory.

Almost every explanation of Kenya's political problems which has been advanced so far has been either explicitly or implicitly based on two key propositions: first, that the small and predominantly British European population numbering about 57,700, together with the heterogeneous Asian and African sectors accounting for approximately 151,900 and 5,902,000 persons respectively, form one common social order; and secondly, that this society may be roughly described as a pyramid in which the dominant Europeans are the apex, the Asians and a few Africans the middle, and the large mass of the Africans the broad base.[2] This description of Kenya's society, though interesting in showing the broad relationship between economic class and racial discrimination, can give a misleading impression: i.e., that increased economic mobility will lead to a lessening of racial discrimination and, therefore, of political tension based on racial grounds. What must be stressed is that in present-day Kenya the racial categories provide the decisive divisions in the political structure. This is not altered by the fact that the Asian group is less identifiable as a politically corporate unit than are the European and African groupings, and that competition for formal power between its religious units occurs both within and without the Asian racial grouping.

Even though economic mobility is increasing within the African and Asian groupings, and the overt signs of racial discrimination may be lessening, there is no indication that Kenya will become socially or politically an integrated society. While social and economic status is determined for each racial group by European standards, social mobility takes place within the substructures of each racial category. Thus social and economic class division is of far less importance than ethnic division. In the territorial or national political scene, therefore, the fundamental

[2] It should be noted that in Kenya, the term "Asian" is generally synonymous with Indians whether they be Muslims or non-Muslims. Arabs are also one of the ethnic components of the population, but they have had no really effective role in power relationships. The population figures quoted in the text are the *de facto* civil population estimates for mid-1956, East African High Commission, *Quarterly Economic and Statistical Bulletin* No. 36 (June, 1957). The Arab population is approximately 33,000 and the overwhelming majority live on the coast.

struggle for power lies between these three politically and constitutionally recognized races, the three distinct groups in Kenya's society which the British Government is attempting to coax into coalition.

In analyzing the various forces reflected in the struggle for political control of Kenya, it must always be kept in mind that the balance of power, legal authority, and responsibility for government rests with Great Britain. It is the British Government that commands the ultimate decisions of policy and in the last resort can provide the armed forces to put down insurrections and maintain security, as in the case of the Mau Mau outbreak. It is the metropolitan government that can make available most of the enormous public capital required for economic development. Furthermore, strategic military considerations on the part of the metropolitan government could have a profound effect on future political and social development.

This paper, however, is fundamentally concerned with the power relationships between the three main racial groups within Kenya around which British policy has evolved. "Power" in this context should be understood as that complex of influences that is exercised in decision-making both formally and informally in Kenya and informally in the United Kingdom. An ethnic group may exercise formal political influence in Kenya by participation in authority in the exercise of public policy; but it may also wield effective control over other groups by extra-constitutional means, i.e., through informal activities which take place outside the formal processes of government. Without politically effective informal influence, in fact, formal influence or the exercise of authority in the political structure is restricted, limited, or impossible to sustain. This does not imply that the basis of informal influence of all groups need necessarily be similar in order to be effective. Nonetheless, both qualitatively and quantitatively there have been and are gross disparities between Europeans, Africans, and Asians in the degree to which they command one or the other of these two types of influences which make up political power in Kenya.

Constitutional Development

Before examining the basis, lines of action, and extent of political power of each of the three groups in Kenya, however, attention must be given to the broad aspects of constitutional development in the post-war period. The Colony and Protectorate of Kenya gained semi-representative government in 1948, when the system of an unofficial majority was introduced in the Legislative Council.[3] But the significance of this constitution lay less in the new relationship established between the legislature and executive, than with the emergence of the issue of "balanced representation." Until 1948, European representation was greater than that accorded to all the non-Europeans. Europeans, Asians, and Arabs each had their own separate electoral rolls, while African representatives were nominated by the Governor from a panel of candidates submitted after informal local council elections. However, with the increase of African representation to four nominated members in 1948, non-European representation equalled that of Europeans. With these minor increases in African representation, the total unofficial membership for the first time exceeded total official membership and, more controversially, reduced the margin of European strength in the Legislative Council to a point which the Europeans considered to be the minimum requirement for the maintenance of their political dominance.

The maintenance of parity, or balanced representation between Europeans and non-Europeans, has been the chief focus of constitutional conflict to date. It dominated the political controversy of 1950-51 when the British Government proposed to increase African and Asian representation in the Legislative Council without any further increase in European participation. European leadership considered that these proposed increases involved a major change in the constitution and thus violated the basis of the allocation of representation established in the 1923 statement of Imperial policy. Advances in African participation had made serious inroads into the European position in the Council since 1923 but none, it was argued, were so fundamental as those so recently announced. While recognizing that some changes in the composition of the Legislative Council would have to be made, the Europeans were unwilling to acquiesce in any alteration which would affect their position of parity of representation with the non-European communities.

After many months of this controversy, the Secretary of State for the Colonies conceded in May, 1951, that no immediate major change would be made in the balance of representation in the Legislative Council.[4] However, it had already been announced in December, 1950,

[3] Royal Instructions 29th March, 1934; as amended by Additional Royal Instructions 20th June, 1935; 27th April, 1948.

[4] 488 H.C. *Debates* 5s, 31 May, 1951, col. 408-410.

that the ultimate objective for Kenya continued to be self-government within the Commonwealth. "Self-government," however, "must include proper provision for all main communities which have made their home in East Africa,"[5] and Africans must be helped forward in their development, so that they might take their full part in the economic and political life of the territory. Ultimate control would be retained by the British Government, it was stated, until the "goal of true partnership" amongst the communities was attained.[6] A constitutional commission representing all communities of Kenya with a neutral chairman from outside the Colony would be appointed within two years to consider the broad issues of political change within this framework of policy. Though the commission was never appointed because of the Emergency, this declaration of policy by the last Labour Government continues to guide British objectives in Kenya.

To give time for consultations on the future constitutional development of the Colony, interim constitutional adjustments were made that did not disturb the proportion of representation on the unofficial side of the Legislative Council.[7] European membership in the Legislative Council was increased from 11 to 14, while that of the Africans was raised from 4 to 6, and of the Asians from 5 to 6 with two of the Asian seats reserved for the separate Muslim Indian electorate. Arab representation remained at two. As soon as a vacancy occurred, an African was to have a seat in the Executive Council, taking the place of the European representing African interests. At the same time, to reduce the disparity between official and unofficial membership, the official membership in the Legislative Council was increased from 16 to 26. These new nominated official members were appointed either from within or without the public services and were drawn from all the main racial groups. They had to subscribe to a general statement of public policy and support Government on any motion of confidence. However, they have been only moderately successful in reflecting territorial rather than ethnic interests and, in fact, though originally criticized for their occasional reluctance to support Government policy, they are now regarded as Government

[5] 482 H.C. *Debates* 5s, 13 December, 1950, col. 1168.

[6] *Ibid.*, col. 1169.

[7] 488 H.C. *Debates* 5s, 31 May, 1951, col. 410. The members of the new Legislative Council took their seats in June, 1952, after the May general election for Asian and European representatives. Additional Royal Instructions bearing dates 21st November, 1951; 14 March, 1952.

members. Nonetheless, this initial method of associating members of the local communities with Government in the Legislative Council continues to be an integral part of Kenya's constitution.

THE GROWTH OF EXECUTIVE GOVERNMENT

Though the constitutional development of the Legislative Council of Kenya has been seriously hindered by ethnic or communal considerations, post-war changes in the executive institutions have produced another avenue for advance. Indeed, the changes that have occurred in executive government provide the most distinctive features of the Kenya constitution.

The association of unofficials with executive government reaches back to 1919 when two Europeans were appointed to the Executive Council. During the Indian-European controversy in the early 1920's, the right of the Asians to one representative was conceded and later a European was appointed to represent African interests. Unable to achieve a European elected majority in the Legislative Council, European leaders focused their attention in the 1930's upon securing greater influence in the area of executive government. In the constitutional changes of 1937, they succeeded in reducing official membership of the Executive Council from eight to four, while their own membership remained at three, including the European representing African interests. Major advances were gained during the war with the expansion of statutory boards under unofficial control. In 1945, the reorganization of the Executive Council and the creation of an embryonic "ministerial system" provided a new and effective method for the expansion of European influence.[8] This system did not restrict the appointment of "ministers" (then called "members") to the Civil Service, but allowed the inclusion of members from the community. However, unofficial representatives in the Legislative Council had to resign their seats in order to accept an appointment. By 1950, two prominent Europeans had become "ministers" in this manner. At one time, indeed, certain European leaders held that this method of participating in executive authority might be a more effective and less controversial way of gaining the essentials of political control than a further attempt to reorganize the Legislative Council in their favor.

---

[8] *Proposals for the Reorganization of the Administration of Kenya.* Sessional Paper No. 3, 1945.

With the development of the "membership system" in the formulation and conduct of public policy, the continuance of the pre-war unofficial representation in executive government, whereby two Europeans, one Asian, and one representative of African interests were members of the Executive Council, proved highly unsatisfactory; for while these representatives could influence executive policy decisions, they continued to be free to oppose these very decisions in the Legislative Council. This fact forced the Government to secure agreement on public policy in a separate meeting of its "ministers" prior to the general meeting of the Executive Council. There was thus an evident need to evolve a responsible system of unofficial participation in executive authority, since the former *ad hoc* methods of government by agreement could no longer meet the demands of an expanding economic and political system. Furthermore, the necessity for immediate reform was dictated by constant criticism by unofficial representatives of Government policy in the conduct of the Emergency.

THE "LYTTELTON" CONSTITUTION [9]

The "Lyttelton" constitution, initiated during the height of the Mau Mau rebellion in early 1954, was drafted to meet these general requirements for responsibility and consent. It embodied the principles of both communal and balanced representation, and an extension of the developing "ministerial system." The political structure of Kenya was altered by introducing a Council of Ministers as the principal instrument of government, even though final authority and responsibility within the territory still rested with the Governor, who in turn was responsible to the Secretary of State for the Colonies. The Council of Ministers originally consisted of fourteen members: six officials who were senior Civil Service officers, two nominated officials appointed from the local community, and six unofficials drawn from the unofficial membership of the Legislative Council, three of whom were elected Europeans, two

[9] *Kenya: Proposals for a Reconstruction of the Government.* (Cmd. 9103) (March, 1954). Provision was also made for not more than five and not less than three parliamentary secretaries, of whom one would be an Arab and two would be Africans. The constitution of the Colony and Protectorate includes the Letters Patent and Royal Instructions, and their amendments and the Secretary of State's despatches of April 15, 1954, and the annexures to those despatches. The unofficial term "Lyttelton" constitution refers in this article to this set of constitutional documents. See *Kenya Official Gazette Supplement* No. 18, 17th April, 1954.

elected Asians, and one a nominated African representative. In October, 1956, provision was made for a fourth European minister and a second African minister.[10] The latter positions were never filled under the "Lyttelton" constitution. However, it may be recognized that the position of parity between European and non-European membership was maintained and that no change in this relationship was made by the "Lennox-Boyd" constitution of November, 1957. It should be noted that in October, 1956, the communal demands of the Arab community were recognized at least partially when provision was made for one Arab representative to attend the Council meetings and, although not technically a member, to have the status of a minister.

The establishment of the Council of Ministers has resulted in the re-emergence of a strong governing majority in the Legislative Council. Since the consequences of communal and balanced representation have prevented advancement towards self-government along traditional lines, this multi-racial constitution has sought to develop an official majority which is in part representative of the local communities. Nonetheless, it is an awkward and difficult situation since the civil servant members derive their authority from the British Government, while the elected members of this governing majority are answerable to their electorates. The elected ministers supposedly act as spokesmen for the section of the population which they represent; but while they may oppose a particular bill at meetings of the Council of Ministers, they must officially side with any decisions taken by this body on the floor of the Legislative Council, since in becoming ministers they must adhere to the principle of collective responsibility for Government policy and thus support the Government in public and in private.

The "Lyttelton" constitution, initiated in April, 1954, was regarded as experimental until a general election for Europeans and Asians could be held to confirm its acceptance by the electorate. This delay in approval of the "Lyttelton" constitution by the European and Asian electorate did not prevent its implementation, for three elected European members, two elected Asians, and one nominated African member of the Legislative Council agreed to cross the floor of the Council and to accept ministerial responsibility. As ministers they had to "agree to refrain from proposing or supporting any legislation concerning the special land rights

[10] *Statement of Constitutional Changes in Kenya.* Nairobi: Press Office Handout No. 959, October 19, 1956. See also *East Africa and Rhodesia,* November 1, 1956.

of the various communities"[11] until the general election of 1960. In order to gain support for these constitutional arrangements, the British Government guaranteed that unless there was prior agreement between Government and the representatives of the main racial groups in the Legislative Council, no change in the communal basis of the franchise, or in the proportion of representatives between the main racial groups would be made in either the Legislative Council or the Council of Ministers until 1960, and that at that time the election would be conducted under the present communal franchise arrangements unless agreement to act otherwise had been reached with all ethnic groups.

An agreement was reached in October, 1956,[12] between the European, Asian, African, and Arab representatives to add two more African representatives to the Legislative Council, and also two corporate representatives nominated by the Governor from names submitted by the European-controlled Board of Agriculture and Board of Industry. These proposals were accepted by the British Government, along with the previously mentioned agreement for one more European and one more African minister. It was further agreed that after the Africans held the first general elections for their eight representatives in March, 1957, more seats should be created in the Legislative Council within the framework of balanced representation which was an integral part of the "Lyttelton" plan. The purpose of these seats was to reduce the disparity between the governmental majority and unofficial representation produced by the "Lyttelton" constitution, and to provide an opportunity for ministers to represent a new arrangement of constituencies rather than the single one from which they were then elected. Regardless of the outcome of these talks, it was agreed that Arab unofficial representation would be increased by one more representative.

The European and Asian general election was held in September, 1956. Had there not been enough elected representatives who were prepared to be ministers, the British Government could have reverted to the constitutional arrangements of 1952 and have taken such other action as was deemed necessary for the conduct of government. This did not happen, however, since the two elected European factions reached an

[11] Colony and Protectorate of Kenya, *Legislative Council Debates*. Vol. LXXI, 13 December, 1956, col. 762-70. A statement by the Chief Secretary on the principle of ministerial responsibility.

[12] *Op. Cit.*, Press Office Handout No. 959.

agreement after the election to recommend three of their group to be nominated by the Governor as ministers. Moreover, Asian cooperation was not in doubt. It thus seemed that the continuance of the "Lyttelton" constitution was ensured.[13]

A constitutional crisis was precipitated, however, by the refusal of the eight newly elected African members to accept the ministerial positions allocated to their community, and by their declaration that the "Lyttelton" constitution was not binding upon them. Government could continue with the appointment of a senior civil servant to the one designated African portfolio, Community Development, but the multiracial character of Government was jeopardized.[14] The spearhead of the African attack was a demand for the reversal of the system of balanced representation in the Legislative Council. They sought either the unconditional granting of African parity of representation with all non-Africans, or a general discussion of the whole "Lyttelton" constitution.[15] An impasse was reached when the Secretary of State for the Colonies refused to consider these demands independently of all other constitutional issues, such as African participation in the Council of Ministers or the direction of future constitutional development. The resignation of the European and Asian ministers during these constitutional discussions in November, 1957, ended the "Lyttelton" constitution and with it the agreement between the representatives of the racial groups of Kenya and the British Government that no constitutional change would be imposed until 1960 without overall consent. The Secretary of State for the Colonies immediately announced that a new constitution would be "imposed."

The failure of the "Lyttelton" constitution demonstrates that the pressing political problem in Kenya lies not in the structure of government but rather in the fundamental issue of power relationships between the three main racial groups. The constitution did not attempt to introduce measures that would alter basic power relationships, but embodied the existing communal structure in the new executive authority. As in

[13] See *East Africa and Rhodesia,* April 18, 1957, for the text of the Governor of Kenya's statement on the continuance of the "Lyttelton" constitution.

[14] With refusal of the African elected members to accept the African portfolio of Community Development, the Governor nominated a senior civil servant to be the minister.

[15] See *The Observer* (London), 28 July, 1957, for a statement of the African demands by Tom Mboya, African member of the Legislative Council for Nairobi.

the past, the primary legitimacy of the constitution was rooted in non-African and particularly in European consent. However, the granting of limited non-European participation in the Council of Ministers recognized the beginning of shared constitutional government, although "standstill" arrangements attempted to prevent further non-European political advance before 1960 without the agreement of European leadership. The "Lyttelton" constitution made provision for an African franchise to elect African representatives to the Legislative Council. This was acted upon, but the newly elected African representatives challenged the balancing principle of European parity of representation and seized from Europeans the initiative for political action.

THE "LENNOX-BOYD" CONSTITUTION[16]

The ending of the "Lyttelton" constitution has neither resulted in a rejection of multi-racial government nor in a fundamental alteration of its basic constitutional principles. Each racial group continues to be represented in both legislative and executive government and the governing majority (composed of senior civil servants, nominated officials, and official and unofficial ministers) is maintained in order that Government may always get its legislation passed even if opposed by all the remaining unofficial elected members. The "constitutional coalition," the Council of Ministers, will continue to have the same number of official and unofficial ministers. The number of ministers assigned to each racial group remains unchanged with four European, two Asian, and two African elected ministers. Two Africans, one Asian, and one Arab are to be added, however, as assistant ministers. Constitutional development thus continues to adhere to the basic principle of associating all the local racial groups with the administration in the formulation and exercise of public policy.

The basic changes in the new "Lennox-Boyd" constitution arise from an attempt to reconcile all the conflicting interests of racial groups within a framework of an evolving multi-racial constitution. The solution sought provides for increased unofficial representation, the establishment of a new system of selection of representatives, and constitutional safeguards.

---

[16] *Kenya: Proposals for New Constitutional Arrangements.* (Cmnd. 309) (November, 1957).

But this endeavor at compromise has not succeeded, for while European, and the majority of Asian leadership has accepted the new constitution, African elected members have rejected it completely.

The heart of the problem is the pursuit of divergent goals by African and European leaders. African leaders have viewed their demands for fifteen new elected seats as a necessary first phase in the ultimate achievement of "one man, one vote" democratic government. European representatives, though recognizing that Africans were under-represented in the Legislative Council, maintain that demands for increased representation cannot be considered in isolation but must include a willingness to participate in the Council of Ministers, and the establishment of adequate safeguards to ensure the future development of multi-racial government. While Africans look to Ghana for their model, Europeans look southward to the Federation of Rhodesia and Nyasaland.

The "Lennox-Boyd" constitution increases African elected representation from eight to fourteen and adds one nominated African, a representative of the Northern Province, to the governmental majority. In addition to these changes, which do not provide for compensated increases in non-African representation, the new Ministry of Housing will become an African portfolio, and that of Adult Education will be added to the present African portfolio of Community Development. With fourteen elected African members, the long-held principle of European parity has been abolished in the Legislative Council, although it continues in the Council of Ministers. When the two corporate seats held by Europeans are removed in 1960, Africans will have equality of representation with the European settler community.

The major objections of Africans to this constitution focus on the proposal for a Council of State and the creation of twelve "selected" members, four from each race, to be elected by the Legislative Council acting as an electoral college, each member exercising a free and secret vote. Candidates for election as "selected" members or, as they will be called, the specially elected members, must be proposed and seconded by members of the Legislative Council, and be supported by three other members. Civil servants who are members of the Legislative Council cannot take part in the nominating process or stand as candidates; with this exception any person either within or without the Legislative Council will be eligible for nomination. Hence, under the present racial composition of the Legislative Council, it would be possible for Africans or

Asians to become specially elected members without the support of the communally elected African or Asian members.[17]

Although the establishment of the Council of State will not introduce a bicameral system of legislation in Kenya, it will nonetheless be an independent body comprising a chairman and ten members drawn from all racial groups and nominated by the Governor. Four of these members will hold office for ten years, three for seven years and three for four years. Members of the Legislative Council will be debarred from concurrent membership of the Council of State. One of its main purposes will be to protect each racial or religious group against discriminatory legislation harmful to its interests. To protect these interests, the Council will have the power to review all legislation, but may only intervene if the proposed law is considered to be differentiating. Such a measure would be one that is disadvantageous to persons of any given racial or religious group, while not being disadvantageous to persons of other such groups. Thus any bill which either directly prejudices persons of one group, or indirectly gives an advantage to persons of another, would be differentiating, and therefore be considered discriminatory.

Two methods of intervention are available to the Council. First, it may delay legislation for a limited period and require the Legislative Council to formally consider its objections. Only after the Council of State has withdrawn its initial objections or the Legislative Council has certified its decision upon a formal report submitted by the Council of State of its objections, may the proposed bill be passed in the Legislative Council. Secondly, even though a bill has been passed, the Council of State may nevertheless make a reasoned request for its reservation on the grounds that the legislation is differentiating. This action may be taken, whether or not the Council of State has previously acted. And unless the Governor is satisfied that it is essential in the public interest that the measure be brought into immediate operation, he will then reserve the measure in accordance with the Council of State's request. Final decision will rest with the Secretary of State for the Colonies whether or not to annul the legislation.[18]

Another important function of the Council of State will be its role

---

[17] "Secretary of State's Despatch," *Kenya Calling: Weekly News Digest:* Nairobi, 15th February, 1958. The specially elected members may not take part in any future nomination process for their seats.

[18] *Ibid.*

in future constitutional change. No further increase in the communally elected representatives will be sanctioned, nor may the racial proportions of the "selected" members be altered within ten years. Consideration may be given, however, to the total increase of the "selected" members and to the system by which they are to be nominated and elected. The latter considerations will be subject to the approval of the Council of State. Thus, in part at least, the role of the British Government as an impartial arbitrator will be transferred to a locally based institution.

Africans have considered this new Council as "unnecessary since the ultimate control of Kenya is still vested in the British Government."[19] Furthermore, they suspect that it will become "an instrument to preserve discrimination and European privileges."[20] Moreover they recognize that the immediate intention in establishing the new "selected" seats is to bring into the Legislative Council four moderate Africans in an effort to preserve multi-racial government. Nonetheless, the hope for this new system of representation is broader: to encourage the growth of territorial rather than purely communal or racial interests, and to provide a first step towards a common roll on a qualitative franchise.

In partially conceding to African demands for greater formal influence in the Legislative Council, the "Lennox-Boyd" constitution has recognized to some degree the shifting power relationships in Kenya. This has not meant the acceptance of a trend towards the emergence of an African-dominated government but, on the contrary, a firm attempt to translate into the constitution the principle that the future government of Kenya should reflect the multi-racial character of its population. Moreover, though the "Lyttelton" constitution initiated multi-racial government, the "Lennox-Boyd" constitution, which will be brought into operation in March and April, 1958, is designed to give greater direction to the achievement of this undefined ideal. In the transitional period ahead, the constitution ensures that an adequate governmental majority will be maintained. Furthermore, the Secretary of State for the Colonies has stated categorically that ultimate control in Kenya will continue to rest with Great Britain "in the foreseeable future."[21]

---

[19] See *East Africa and Rhodesia,* November 21, 1957, for the full text of statement issued by the African Elected Members Organization.

[20] *Ibid.*

[21] *The Times* (London), November 9, 1957.

LOCAL GOVERNMENT

Not only central but also local government institutions reflect the ethnic composition of the population and the differential in their degree of formal and informal influence. Communal participation has been most significant in the Municipal Council of Nairobi and in the governing bodies of some urban areas. African district councils function in the main as local agencies of the central government with varying degrees of responsibility. In the European settled areas, county councils based on English local government practice are overwhelmingly European bodies and appear reluctant to accept any influential non-European participation. Local bodies have been of secondary importance in the struggle for political power in Kenya, for all politically conscious leadership groups recognize the central government as the locus of power and authority. Thus the early development of substantial European parliamentary power has had a profound effect in teaching the importance of participation in central government institutions.

The Dominant Role of the European

To turn now to an analysis of existing power relationships in Kenya, it is clear that the group that wields the greatest political power in that country is the European colonists, despite the fact that they are outnumbered by more than 100 to 1.[22] This power is derived chiefly from their economic superiority over Asians and Africans, and from their strategic cultural and personal links with Great Britain.

The economic superiority of the European settler is due fundamentally to the greater technical skill and education with which he is endowed, as well as the sizeable capital at his disposal. Technical skill means that, unlike the Asian or the African, the European settler is able to organize production in accordance with modern scientific methods. The large amount of capital at his disposal ensures his ability to achieve economies of scale as, for example, in the formation of large and efficient cooperative societies which serve to market Kenya's products in foreign countries.

22 British Colonial Civil Servants are included in the demographic estimates of the European population. Since some of these Civil Servants retire in Kenya and some of the local European population are now members of the Civil Service, no clear delineation can be made between the permanent and non-permanent sectors of the European population. It is roughly estimated, however, that the permanent European sector is about 30,000.

In short, technical skill and capital are the factors which make the European economically far more efficient and productive than either the Asian or the African, and have enabled him to achieve such a position of political dominance in the internal affairs of Kenya. In turn, this dominance has enabled the European to strengthen his economic position, particularly in times of crisis through the provision of credit, special facilities, and privileges.

These assets have also enabled the European generally to enjoy a distinctive way of life and a much higher standard of living than the other two groups. Incomes and wages reflect the significant differential between ethnic groups. The average white wage is about double that of the Asian and several times higher than that of the African. The center of Kenya's agricultural development lies in the upland country, an area in which ninety percent of the population lives, and the European has succeeded in legally reserving about one-third of this valuable land for his exclusive ownership and use. In addition, Europeans control the largest proportion of commerce, mining, and industry.

Europeans have thus achieved a position of economic predominance during the last half century which they wish to maintain, consolidate, and expand. This purpose has been well served by the color bar, which has been so striking a feature of Kenya's social structure. It has been used to prevent non-European settlement in the White Highlands and, until World War II, to restrict African production of certain cash crops. It has been employed to restrict Asian competition in many major spheres of economic activity. A legally sanctioned wage and salary structure which, for equivalent jobs, specifies different pay rates for different ethnic groups, functioned in the recent past to provide varying patterns of incentives in the allocation of labor within each ethnic group. These legal sanctions have had far-reaching influence, but custom and behavior patterns have also acted to protect the European wage earner.

The cultural heritage of the European has given him a distinct advantage in the pursuit of political power within Kenya's formal structure of authority, based as it is on British traditions, values, and techniques. The ability to organize political action which is effective in the constitutional structure, easy access to and influence over persons holding positions of authority both locally and in Great Britain, the facilities to publicize and communicate the settlers' point of view, the appeal to "kith and kin" in the Mother Country, and an intimate knowledge of the rules of the political system, have all contributed immensely to the achievement of European political power.

Considering themselves the political and social elite, and the heirs presumptive to British authority, the continued attempt of the Europeans to control all situations has provided the outstanding features of the political history of the territory.[23] Precedents and myths, in part rooted in political victories, long fostered a European belief that complete political control was feasible as an ultimate goal. As an educated elite group reared in British traditions, they considered it their "natural right" to demand the transplanting of institutions of responsible government, and in this respect found considerable support in the past among Governors of Kenya. Disregarding the ethnic and cultural features of Kenya, and the increasingly influential pressures for more consideration of African rights, Kenya Europeans bolstered their claims by pointing to the political development of the white Dominions and to the grant of self-government to Southern Rhodesia in 1923.

The constitutional and political development of Kenya from a Protectorate to the present multi-racial government, is largely a result of this European drive for political power which strove to achieve as large a role as possible in the political system in the pre-World War II period and since then has been seeking to consolidate and entrench its position. Out of political conflict both with Asians and the Imperial Power, the Europeans have become a self-conscious group with common political interests and a belief that European unity is essential for effective political action. There has thus been a marked degree of consensus within the European group that the emergence of separate European parties after 1952 weakened the political effectiveness of the group as a whole. Conflict with other ethnic groups and with the British Government has

[23] *British Policy in Kenya Colony* (New York, 1937), by Marjorie Ruth Dilley, is a comprehensive and well-documented study covering the period 1900 to 1935. See Elspeth Huxley, *White Man's Country,* 2 Vols. (London, 1935), for a study of white settlement from the viewpoint of white colonists. See also W. K. Hancock, *Survey of British Commonwealth Affairs,* Vol. 1, pp. 209-237, for a study of the Indian question. Compare M. F. Hill, *The Dual Policy in Kenya* (Nairobi, 1944); S. and K. Aaronovith, *Crisis in Kenya* (London, 1947), an analysis of the Kenya situation from a left-wing point of view; W. McGregor Ross, *Kenya From Within — A Short Political History* (London, 1927) and Norman M. Leys, *Kenya* (London, 1924) which are both critical of white colonists and Government policy. See also Elspeth Huxley and Margery Perham, *Race and Politics in Kenya* (London, 1956), a debate between the authors on various aspects of the Kenya situation.

helped to maintain the exclusive identity of the Europeans as an elite group, for whom the White Highlands are important as a prestige symbol. Thus the Highlands have a political significance beyond their economic value.

In his struggle for political power, the European has achieved some outstanding successes. His dominance in the political system was institutionalized with the adoption of disproportionate communal representation in 1923.[24] His formal influence within the parliamentary system has been expanded and so far protected from decisive non-European encroachment. In addition to the four European elected members in the present Council of Ministers, there have been, since 1946, at least one and at times two European settlers holding executive government portfolios as nominated officials. Their position is further strengthened through the influential roles that Europeans perform on governmental committees and statutory boards. An example of the informal influence that the European has effectively employed both locally and in the United Kingdom was the withdrawal by the Labour Government in 1947 of their proposal for equality of ethnic representation in the proposed Central Assembly of the East Africa High Commission after a year of intense European opposition.[25] So significant, in fact, has European influence been in certain periods that Lord Hailey wrote in the 1930's that these "interests have exercised an influence on policy hardly less than they might have attained under a fully developed form of responsible government."[26]

Nevertheless, European ambitions have been thwarted by a combination of factors beyond their control. Among these factors have been the ability of Asians in the early days of white settlement to appeal to the Imperial Power as citizens of the British Empire; in more recent years, rising African dissent and their rejection of presumptive control; and the increasing reluctance of the Imperial Power to relinquish its moral trusteeship, and therefore its authority. The latter fact demonstrates that no clearly defined community of interests has existed between the

---

[24] See *Indians in Kenya: A Memorandum.* (Cmd. 1922) (1923) for a statement on the acceptance of communal representation.

[25] Compare *Inter-territorial Organization in East Africa.* Col. No. 191, 1945 and *Inter-territorial Organization in East Africa.* Col. No. 210, 1947.

[26] Lord Hailey, *An African Survey* (London, 1938), p. 383. See also *Reports of the Commission on Closer Union of the Dependencies in Eastern and Central Africa.* (Cmd. 3234) (1929), p. 89.

Imperial Power and the European settler group, and reflects the essentially empirical character of British colonial policy in Kenya.

The Limited Political Role of the Asian

The Asian population has never exercised decisive informal or formal influence in the political system. As a predominantly urbanized immigrant community restricted essentially to trading and the pursuit of various crafts and professions, they have had to adapt themselves to an agricultural economy and to an administrative system dominated by Europeans. Though recognized by the administration as one of the major component racial groups of Kenya, their internal structure reflects no such implied unity for social action. Their two major subdivisions of Muslim and non-Muslim have been accorded political status within the Asian category in the post-war period, and other factional groups such as the Sikhs and Ismailia Muslims have obtained their own representatives among the nominated official members of the Legislative Council. In the recent constitutional change Arabs are included, at least partially in the Asian category, in the granting to them of one of the four "selected" seats reserved for Asians. But while the social and political organization of the Asian is far more complex than is generally conceived, the balance and adjustments of representation in the political system continue to regard Asians as one of the three major racial categories in Kenya politics.

Asian political power has been declining in the post-war period in relation both to that of the European and of the African. The system of communal representation has critically limited Asian influence in the decision-making process of central and local government. Asian membership in the councils of central government has never been more than half that of the European settler and is now less than that of the African in the Legislative Council. The portfolio assigned to one of the two Asian ministers does not compare in significance to any of those held by Europeans. Abolition of the India Office has deprived the Asians of a valuable ally in any attempt to influence the British Government. Any appeals to the India of today would only confirm European and African anxiety over the Asian's divided territorial loyalties. What informal influence the Asian exerts in challenging European dominance has been essentially based on the doctrine of equal political and social opportunities for all. But though Asian political organizations have in the past employed techniques of political boycott, and attempted in the immediate post-war years to achieve African political alliances, neither of these approaches has proved fruitful in advancing their own interests.

At the minimum, Asians seek to retain their formal influence within the parliamentary system in relation to other races. Under the "Lyttelton" constitution, Asian representatives have been able to play at least a limited role of influence in the shifting power relationships between Europeans and Africans. Asians have in the past seen their main interests linked to those of the European and have sought acceptance within the oligarchy. There are, however, some indications that in the future the majority of Asians may see their interests best served by supporting the cause of African nationalism.

Quite apart from a potential displacement of their formal influence by emerging African political power, the Asians' limited social solidarity has acted either to restrict or diffuse their political strength. Their opposition to European dominance still provokes some lingering cohesion, but racial isolation, and the social and religious conflicts that this isolation helps to promote, have reduced the possibility of substantial and sustained unified political action. Religion is predominant as the basis for social and political organization. Despite the efforts of the Kenya Indian Congress, and its predecessor, to maximize Asian political strength, disparate religious affiliations hinder in large measure their ability to present a united political front in opposition to European power. Moreover, the Asians' marginal social position in a white-dominated Kenya has yielded few positions of prestige and status. As a result, competition among Asian leaders has been keen, and they have approached their religious groups to support their political aspirations. Thus the Sikhs and Muslims have sought separate representation in the Colony's parliamentary system, and the Muslims succeeded in 1952 in obtaining two elected representatives to the Legislative Council.[27] Furthermore, one of the two Asian ministries is designated for the Muslims. Paradoxically, it seems that European racial policies have for the most part fostered more dissension than unity amongst the Asians, and European settlers have not hesitated to exploit the religious and social divisions of this heterogeneous racial grouping.

[27] "The Report of the Committee on Indian Electoral Representation," Colony and Protectorate of Kenya, *Legislative Council Debates,* 13, 14, 18 December 1951, col. 1024-1028, 1075-1094.

Changing Political Role of the African

Although the Imperial Power declared African interests to be paramount in 1923, this declaration did not affect the political power structure of Kenya or lead to any radical departures in the formulation and conduct of policy.[28] Indeed, in retrospect this declaration appears to have been rather a moral principle than a basis for practical politics. Now, however, a goal of racial partnership in the parliamentary system has replaced the earlier doctrine.

Not until the post-war period has the African been able to modify power relationships established in the initial years of white settlement, and even today he does so more by virtue of his recognized potential, than by mobilized political action. Until 1944 Africans had no direct participation in the central government's legislative or executive institutions. It was maintained that his interests were best served by the two specially selected European members and by those in constitutional authority directly concerned in native administration. What direct participation the African had in representative organs of government was limited to African local councils, which essentially served as local agencies of central government though with restricted responsibility. Moreover, the nominated then predominated over the elected members in these councils. Through incipient political and social associations, Africans achieved a degree of informal influence by making known their needs and disabilities to those British civil servants, visiting commissions, missionaries, and other elements in Kenya and in England who recognized the Africans' lack of political power to protect their own interests. However, at that time European power and, to a lesser extent, Asian demands for equality of status, constituted the main factors which the metropolitan government had to consider in the government of Kenya. African political associations, such as the Kikuyu Central Association, were considered as subversive and disloyal in challenging the basis of responsibility and authority. The governmental ideal was the maintenance of the conditions for a stable political oligarchy.

The post-war period has witnessed both legal and non-legal African political action to gain substantial formal influence in the parliamentary system. The chief demands in the immediate post-war years were for direct representation in municipal councils, increase of powers for

---

[28] *Indians in Kenya: A Memorandum.* (Cmd. 1922) (1923).

district councils, increased representation in the Legislative Council, and the direct election of these African representatives. Before being proscribed in April, 1953, the Kenya African Union, which had achieved a membership well over 100,000, demanded African parity of unofficial representation in the Legislative Council and a common electoral roll for all ethnic groups.[29] These demands have only been fulfilled in part, but more extensive ones are now being pressed by the first elected African representatives.

Though the African nominated members who represented African interests until March, 1957, were allowed considerable latitude in their criticism of Government, they could claim only a partially expressed African mandate and thus exercised little formal influence in the conduct of public policy. In 1952, an African was appointed to the Executive Council; under the "Lyttelton" constitution, one of their number was a member of the Council of Ministers and held the portfolio of Community Development — essentially an African matter not affecting the vital interests of the European population. Even today, the portfolios assigned to the two African ministerial positions do not grant executive responsibility over matters of vital interest to all races. And while the removal of European parity in the Legislative Council constitutes a significant African political advance, the retention of European parity in the Council of Ministers is a recognition of the true locus of power and authority.

Although African representation in the central government councils has expanded in the post-war period, the outstanding political achievement is the introduction of an African electoral roll. The first African direct election took place in March, 1957, for the selection of eight African representatives by means of a qualified multi-vote scheme which enfranchised Kikuyu of sworn loyalty and an estimated fifty per cent of the adult non-Kikuyu African population. Though only 126,508 voters were registered, and the electoral districts, except for Nairobi, covered large areas, approximately 79 per cent of the voters cast their ballot.[30] The most significant result of the election was that all the

[29] "Kenya African Union Statement, 27 October 1952," reproduced in *Opportunity in Kenya:* Fabian Publications Ltd., Research Series No. 162, Appendix I. See *The Times,* 5 March 1951. See also Letter to Editor, *The Times,* 11 June 1952, by Mr. Mbiyu Koinange, Delegate in Great Britain of the Kenya African Union.

[30] A summary of the results of the First African Election may be found in *East Africa and Rhodesia,* March 21, 1957. The limited qualified franchise based on age, educa-

sitting representatives, many of whom had been members for several years, were defeated, with the exception of two who had been appointed by the Governor only a few months earlier.

The newly elected members did not hesitate to voice their joint objection to the principle of European parity and the continuance of the "Lyttelton" constitution. Not one of their number was prepared to accept either of the two ministerial positions set aside for Africans in the Council of Ministers. At each parliamentary opportunity, they launched attacks on the lack of adequate representation in municipal local bodies, restrictions on African political organizations and meetings, social discrimination and basic government policies. The disappearance of European parity in the Legislative Council in the new constitution is their first major success. Mr. Tom Mboya, the Member for Nairobi and apparent leader of the African representatives, has emphatically defined their ultimate goal to be "a society and Government in which people, regardless of race or colour, shall be regarded as individuals, and not closely-knit racial groups or communities, and that all individuals shall be equals, enjoying equal rights and opportunities."[31]

At the same time, weakness of the African is reflected not only in his limited share in the formal processes of central government, but also in the small informal influence which he exerts in the social order. Lacking technical skill, education, and capital, the African plays a subordinate role in the market economy. The poverty of many African land units, together with the low African wage scale and limited educational opportunities further contribute to his economic insecurity and limited mobility. Socially, the African has only a peripheral position in a social order whose norms, standards, and values are European, and his contacts with the European are essentially limited to economic, political, and ceremonial necessities. Since he is not assimilated into European society, he does not have access to important positions of informal influence, while racial attitudes further limit his access to positions of prestige and wealth. Moreover, the African must compete for political power in a system alien to his cultural background, and with an inadequate command of the techniques and facilities of that system.

---

tion, experience, public service, and character, provides that an elector may earn up to three votes. See further *Ibid.*, February 7, 1957, for brief biographies of the 37 candidates.

[31] *East Africa and Rhodesia,* April 4, 1957.

Tribal parochialism further acts to restrict the political effectiveness of the African population.[32] There are numerous tribal and subtribal groups, among all of whom the consciousness of separate identity is prominent. The tribe has not only continued to be the focus of individual loyalty and identity, but social and political changes in Kenya have re-enforced the separatism of each tribe as a local community. Though the politically significant agricultural tribes, such as the Kikuyu, Meru, Embu and Luo, the Coastal and Nyanza Bantu, who constitute the vast majority of the population, had no structural or technical basis of differentiation, they also had only limited common political or economic interests. Migrants from one Bantu tribal group to another could be absorbed permanently or temporarily, but few lasting links were established between the tribes. With the arrival of British administration and white settlement, the boundaries of these separate agricultural tribes were fixed and given permanence through a tribal reserve system.

Moreover these tribal units became the primary focus of administration and policy. The government appointed chiefs and headmen from the tribe as agents of control; courts were created which administered customary law and there were no possibilities of developing inter-tribal law. Eventually local native councils were established, now known as African district councils, but the majority of these embrace only a single tribal area. Primary and intermediate schools are at the local level, and only contribute in a limited degree to a trans-tribal consciousness. Political and social associations have also existed, but these have been essentially tribal, and have only re-enforced the tribal orientation of the overwhelming majority of Africans. Moreover, the treating of each tribal group more or less separately in the allocation of revenue and services has contributed to local solidarity and tribal competition, particularly since only a limited amount of public revenue is available for African development. Conflict situations arising out of these and other factors, such as limited work opportunities, tend to foster local cohesion and to help prevent the spread of a trans-tribal consciousness.

The economic organization of Kenya has also fostered tribal parochialism through the existence of a dual economy. Both Europeans and Asians are engaged in the production and marketing of products but the overwhelming proportion of Africans are predominantly committed to

---

[32] See the *East Africa Royal Commission 1953-1955 Report* (Cmd. 9475) (1955) for a study of the problems of African economic and social development.

the subsistence sector of the economy. A large number of Africans have a temporary and intermittent association with the market economy, but only a very few of them become permanently detached from the tribal areas. Customary and quasi-legal racial discrimination among and within occupations, supported by a wide disparity in educational and training opportunities, has acted to limit the vertical mobility of Africans. Moreover within the tribal subsistence economy, administrative controls are frequently so designed that whatever encouragement they give to the expansion of cash-cropping and marketing is differentiated along individual tribal lines. Tribal or sub-tribal self-sufficiencies are important secondary objectives. Thus traditional institutions, like the indigenous system of land tenure and kinship obligation, have usually been disturbed as little as possible. The result is that fragmentation of Kenya along tribal lines is perpetuated in this economic structure. What has been slowly emerging, therefore, is a disparate collection of segmented, and basically non-competing tribal groups. Under such conditions individual interests and loyalties remain with the tribe.

Despite these weaknesses in formal and informal influences, incipient African nationalism is a potential source of African political power and the greatest threat to continued European ascendancy. To date, its development has been inhibited not only by tribal parochialism, but also by the small number of educated English-speaking Africans and the inadequacies of social communication which would enable them to function as a national elite. The history in the post-war period of the Kenya African Union, their first large-scale political movement, vividly illustrates the structural weaknesses of this mass political movement in terms of trans-tribal nationalism. Though the Kenya African Union realized the necessity of maintaining trans-tribal membership in its central executive, and the leadership of Jomo Kenyatta commanded territorial recognition by Africans, there was little politically conscious non-Kikuyu leadership, and few facilities for organization for rapid and continuous communication within and between the major African rural areas. Only amongst the Kikuyu were the requisites of leadership and social communication sufficiently developed to support mass political mobilization. It is not surprising that as the Kenya African Union developed out of a small-scale organization, led initially by a trans-tribal elite, into a mass movement, its leadership and organization became primarily Kikuyu; and that its orientation and appeal made use of symbols, slogans, and values derived essentially from Kikuyu culture which had limited effectiveness in the non-Kikuyu areas.

Historically, the initial impact of Western civilization on African life has been greater and had a more profound effect among the Kikuyu than among the other tribes.[33] Hemmed in between the Aberdare mountains and the areas of European settlement, they have experienced intense European contact. From the very early days of European immigration, the land reserves of the Kikuyu extended into the suburbs of Nairobi; as time went on this proximity to Kenya's major urban center brought increasing numbers of Kikuyus into varying degrees of association with the European market economy. But greater contact also brought in its wake greater discontent. European contact was largely responsible for increasing population pressure on Kikuyu reserves, the boundaries of which had been rigidly fixed by Government action, and employment opportunities within the European market economy were never sufficient to offset the many acute problems caused by shortage of land. Greater contact with Europeans also meant more frequent exposure to discriminatory treatment. Discontent was therefore greater among the Kikuyu than among other tribes and made them more susceptible to organization in a mass political movement. All that was needed was adequate leadership.

The emergence of political leadership among the Kikuyu was provided by a number of favorable conditions. One important element was the post-war growth in communications and transportation. A large number of vernacular newspapers appeared, a few of which achieved large circulations. People could move easily and quickly between Kikuyu country and Nairobi, and meetings were held whose attendance reached into thousands. Among the Kikuyu there had developed numerous groups of voluntary associations which were able to accelerate the process of mass organization. The independent schools and the African churches helped considerably in the movement, because these groups cut across

[33] See J. C. Carothers, *The Psychology of Mau Mau* (Nairobi, 1954). Compare the impressions of a journalist, Negley Farson, *Last Chance in Kenya* (London, 1951), pp. 107-112, for a report of the Kiambu district; Patrick Monkhouse, "The Mau Mau in Kenya," *Manchester Guardian,* 12 November 1952, 17 November 1952, 18 November 1952, 20 November 1952, 24 November 1952. See also L. S. B. Leakey, *Mau Mau and the Kikuyu,* (London, 1953), pp. 57-86, for the impact of European penetration.

traditional clan and local loyalties.[34] They helped the fostering of wider concepts of Kikuyu and African unity.

The development of militant nationalism was further accelerated once there was a widespread rejection of any justification for the existing distribution of economic, social and political rights and privileges. Neither the political nor the social order of Kenya was considered by the majority of Kikuyu to be any longer legitimate. However, the movements that developed failed to acquire the character of a positive drive for the achievement of an African political society or a nation state. And this was due in no small measure to the lack of trans-tribal contact. Debarred from meaningful participation in the European-dominated political order, and with their leaders impressed by the effectiveness of European political action, these movements and, in particular, Mau Mau, tended to become secretive, conspiratorial, and insurrectionary.

The New Context of Political Conflict

In this analysis emphasis has been put so far upon the conditions which have inhibited the development of African political power. But attention must also be directed to some of the factors and trends now prevailing or emerging in Kenya which are reshaping power relationships.

Of outstanding importance has been the emergence of a trans-tribal elite and an infrastructure of nationalism in terms both of potential territorial organization and communication. Of particular significance has been the social and political development of the Luo people of Nyanza, who are second in size to the Kikuyu. Together, the Kikuyu and Luo constitute approximately forty-five per cent of the African population of Kenya. Strategically important in this respect are the increasing numbers of Luo who have some degree of college education, the organization of the Luo Union as the largest and most active tribal union in East Africa, and the consciousness of the majority of Luo political leaders of the need for trans-tribal political action. Today, members of the Luo tribe hold key positions of leadership in the African trade unions and in Nairobi political organizations. Three of the eight elected African members of the Legislative Council are Luo and their

[34] See George Bennett, "The Development of Political Organization in Kenya," *Political Studies*. Vol. V, No. 2, June, 1957.

apparent leader, Mr. Tom Mboya, is a Luo. No doubt the neutralization of Kikuyu leadership during the Emergency has helped the rapid emergence of Luo leadership into prominence. But in this respect it is significant that Luo leaders have been extremely cautious in their explanations of Mau Mau to avoid criticizing the former dominant political role of Kikuyu leadership. In fact they have been very conscious of the need for trans-tribal political cooperation and have viewed African social and political development primarily in territorial rather than in tribal terms. Apart from their immediate demands for a larger formal role for Africans in the central government, the Luo leaders have also made a conscious attempt to emphasize the ideology of individual equality.

Although stress has been placed upon the new political role of the Luo, it should not be implied that other tribal groups are devoid of educated leadership or organization. Not only are political leadership roles beginning to be held by individuals who had no, or only limited, contact with politics in the past, but the total number of Africans with overseas university training is increasing yearly. It has been estimated that by 1960 they will number approximately 200, while several hundred more will have had advanced training at Makerere College. Already an important nucleus of such leadership exists in the urban and rural areas, forming an important new factor in power relationships. Furthermore, there has developed within the majority of African rural areas an important secondary level of leadership: men who have attained varying degrees of education and who function as communicators and organizers in their respective areas. Outside the Luo rural areas, organization is at present weak or limited, but both the legal and social opportunities for its development are changing.

At the moment, Government policy does not permit the formation of territorial-wide African political movements, although district African political organizations are allowed outside the Kikuyu land unit. This prohibition functions not only to prevent the emergence of a mass political movement, but also to restrict organizational opportunities to the tribal level. Since nearly all African electoral constituencies embrace more than one district, it even acts to prevent a single dominant organization within a constituency. Further restrictions, under a system of licensing, control all political meetings of Africans both as to where they may be held and who may address the meeting.

Nonetheless, the granting of the franchise to Africans provides a constitutional vehicle for political education and action, and gives meaning and sanction to the views of African representatives. The events of the last year have demonstrated the strong parliamentary position that direct election has brought the African in the Legislative Council. At the same time the very restriction of the African to a separate electoral roll serves to encourage thinking and action along racial lines. By further compartmentalizing political action in Kenya, it more sharply defines the struggle for political power and tends to re-inforce the sentiments of racial consciousness which are generated by a common African opposition to the dominant non-African minority. Moreover, the franchise provides African leaders with opportunities to use the African's numerical strength as a political tool in the achievement of political power.

Though only a nascent and imperfectly mobilized political consciousness now exists among the African mass, factors of change are at work. Already a trans-tribal elite is in process of formation which will be capable of furnishing the leadership to its respective areas in the development of a congress-type political movement. Moreover, the acceleration of factors of social change represented by economic development in both urban and rural areas, and the expansion of educational facilities on all levels are increasing the spatial and vertical mobility of the African population. These trends, together with an increasing weakening of the traditional African societies and sanctions will release a growing number of individuals who are susceptible to the mass mobilization of this emerging elite.

At least two alternatives might fulfill the ambitions and aspirations of this elite. The first is that Europeans would immediately allow the emerging African elite to achieve positions of prestige and status, and to share equally the formal power of the parliamentary system in making decisions over all major aspects of political and economic life. The second alternative is that the African elite mobilize the African mass for the purpose of displacing the European from his present commanding position of power. This process of creating a territorial political movement might well be facilitated by the skillful exploitation of existing social and economic inequalities, and by linking tribal and district political associations through their leaders into a country-wide organization.

Furthermore, the African elite could conceivably strengthen its position by an appeal to the ideology and principle of democracy which would find a sympathetic response in Great Britain and elsewhere.

If the Europeans were to accept the first alternative of penetration by the African elite into the political power structure, there would be a slight possibility that they might succeed in detaching the African elite from a potential nationalist movement. Some form of joint European and African oligarchy would have at least short-term possibilities. But Europeans have already recognized that this would be but the first step in a further expansion of African political power. It is significant that though European leadership has become politically divided in the last five years, this division has not centered around basic goals or objectives, but has related to tactics, procedures, and means for maintaining and entrenching European formal influence in Kenya. Clearly, the European settler is disposed to resist any constitutional reform that recognizes a decline in his formal influence in the parliamentary system. Thus it can be anticipated that the African elite will be driven to exploit the possibilities of African nationalism.

Since the logic of the situation seems to compel a more hardened European political response toward African political aspirations, while at the same time the African elite is driven to mobilize the African population to advance their own political interests, uncompromising ideologies are likely to gain wider appeal in the future. Because of its political weakness, the Asian group can play only a minor role as third force. It is quite likely, therefore, that the future will see an increasing polarization in the power struggle within Kenya. This is a possibility which bodes ill for the development of a stable political community, since in such a political atmosphere liberal and moderate views will find few supporters.

The clash of divergent interests between Europeans and Africans has resulted in the rejection of the "Lyttelton" constitution because shifting power relationships could not be accommodated in the constitution without agreement by all racial groups. The "Lennox-Boyd" constitution recognizes the need to grant the African a larger role in the exercise of formal influence, but equally important, it seeks to ensure not merely the immediate continuance of multi-racial government, but its future acceptance. Though political conflict has led to a constitution which seeks a wider basis of consent, it has also brought into focus the wide gulf that exists between Africans and Europeans over basic matters of political principle and objectives.

Multi-racial government may be initially accepted by both Africans and Europeans so long as it does not explicitly deny their political aspirations. It would, therefore, be unrealistic to consider the "Lennox-Boyd" constitution as other than transitional. Peaceful political change involves the reconciliation of claims of competing interests; however, this is only possible in a progressive society held together by a common basis of loyalties. A critical difficulty of Kenya is the absence of such a system of loyalties, and the fact that Europeans now associate themselves with maintaining the established order and rest their case on the present legal arrangements. Africans seeking political and social change directed towards the achievement of majority rule in government challenge not only these legal arrangements, but the legitimacy of the established order itself.

In order to provide a means of channeling the conflict of interests and the struggle for power into avenues of peaceful change, Great Britain may have to abandon its traditional policy of "empiricism." The major weakness of the present policy of "empiricism" is that it intensifies racial politics and creates doubts and fears among all contending groups as to their future roles in a self-governing state. Where the Imperial Power is dealing with a society which is more or less integrated, the pursuit of *ad hoc* policies is likely to aid the processes of nationalism and thus reinforce common loyalties. In a racially diverse territory like Kenya, where there exists deep insecurity as to the nature of future political authority, the failure to declare explicitly and precisely the general principles on which the constitution of the self-governing state will be based, leads only to increasing suspicion among the groups of one another and of the Imperial Power. Furthermore, a declaration of explicit political and social goals may be needed not only to meet the immediate political problems ahead, but also to lay a basis for future democratic parliamentary government. The political course of events in Kenya since the last war strongly suggests that, in the absence of such a declaration, the gap between aspirations and reform may become so wide that a common loyalty to Kenya will become impossible.

BIBLIOGRAPHY

This somewhat extensive bibliography is designed not merely as a guide to additional material on the specific problems considered in the papers of this volume but also as an aid to students concerned with the broader aspects of government and politics in Ghana, Nigeria, Central Africa and Kenya. Important general political studies of British Africa are listed together as these are relevant to the problems in more than one territory.

The bibliography is of necessity selective. Though the emphasis is upon government and politics, studies in anthropology and economics have been included since they contain material essential to the study of African governments and political change. The selection emphasizes contemporary studies and is influenced, to some extent, by the availability of material to American students. The bibliographies listed at the beginning give some guide to further reading. Many of the books have their own bibliographies; for example, the volumes in the *Ethnographic Survey of Africa* contain useful listings of the literature relevant to the area of the survey. Some of the more significant newspapers and journals of direct value in studying political developments are given for each territory as well as for British Africa as a whole.

Continuing official reports are not listed, though it must be kept in mind that they are important sources of information. The Colonial Office publishes annual reports of Nigeria, Nyasaland, Northern Rhodesia, and Kenya, and did so for the Gold Coast until its independence. Similarly, the Colonial Office submits annual reports to the United Nations on the Trust Territory of the Cameroons and, until its incorporation with Ghana, on Togoland. Within each territory, the annual reports of each government department contain much information, some of which, such as those on African Affairs, are of special value. Finally, reference should be made to the Debates in the British Parliament on African questions which are digested in the quarterly *Journal of the Parliaments of the Commonwealth,* and to the Debates in the African territorial legislatures. These Debates, which are published and available through the respective Government Printers, are extremely useful since they contain background information and a wide-ranging array of fact and opinion on legislation, political issues, and questions of government policy.

BIBLIOGRAPHIES

CARDINALL, A. W. *A Bibliography of the Gold Coast.* Accra: Government Printer, 1932.

COLEMAN, JAMES S. "A Survey of Selected Literature on the Government and Politics of British West Africa", *The American Political Science Review,* Vol. 49, No. 4, December 1955, pp. 1130-50.

COMHAIRE, J. *Urban Conditions in Africa.* Select reading list. London: Oxford University Press, for the Institute of Colonial Studies, 1952.

CONOVER, HELEN. *Africa South of the Sahara.* A selected, annotated list of writings, 1951-1956. Washington: Library of Congress, General Reference and Bibliography Division, 1957.

FORDE, DARYLL, ed. *Select Annotated Bibliography of Tropical Africa.* Compiled by the International African Institute for the Twentieth Century Fund. New York, June 1956.

MEEK, C. K. *Colonial Law.* A bibliography with special reference to native African systems of law and land tenure. London: Oxford University Press, for Nuffield College, 1948.

PERHAM, MARGERY. *Colonial Government.* Annotated reading list on British Colonial Government. London: Oxford University Press, for Nuffield College, 1950.

PERRY, RUTH. *A Preliminary Bibliography of the Literature of Nationalism in Nigeria.* London: The International African Institute, 1956.

YOUNG, R. and LIEBENOW, JR., J. G. "Survey of Background Material for the Study of Government in East Africa", *American Political Science Review,* Vol. 48, No. 1, March 1954, pp. 187-203.

BRITISH AFRICA GENERAL

BROWN, WILLIAM O., *ed. Contemporary Africa: Trends and Issues. The Annals of the American Academy of Political and Social Science,* Vol. 298, March 1955.

BUELL, RAYMOND L. *The Native Problem in Africa.* 2 vols. New York: Macmillan, 1928.

COLEMAN, JAMES S. "Nationalism in Tropical Africa", *American Political Science Review,* Vol. 47, No. 2, June 1954, pp. 404-26.

COLEMAN, JAMES S. "Problems of Political Integration in Emergent Africa", *Western Political Quarterly,* Vol. 8, No. 1, March 1955, pp. 44-57.

CROCKER, W. R. *Self-Government for the Colonies.* London: Allen and Unwin, 1949.

ELIAS, T. OLAWALE. *The Nature of African Customary Law.* Manchester: Manchester University Press, 1956.

FORTES, M. and EVANS-PRITCHARD, E. E., *ed. African Political Systems.* London: Oxford University Press, for the International African Institute, 1950. (First published 1940.)

GLUCKMAN, MAX. *Custom and Conflict in Africa.* Oxford: Blackwell, 1955.

HAILEY, LORD. *An African Survey.* Revised 1956. London: Oxford University Press, 1957. (First published 1938.)

HAILEY, LORD. *Native Administration and Political Development in British Tropical Africa.* Report to the Secretary of State for the Colonies, 1940-42. London: H.M.S.O.

HAILEY, LORD. *Native Administration in the British African Territories.* 5 vols. London: H.M.S.O., 1950-1953.

HAINES, C. GROVE, *ed. Africa Today.* Baltimore: The Johns Hopkins Press, 1955.

HANCOCK, W. K. *Survey of British Commonwealth Affairs.*
Vol. I. *Problems of Nationality 1918-1936.* London: Oxford University Press, 1937.

Vol. II. *Problems of Economic Policy 1918-1939*. London: Oxford University Press, 1942.

THE HANSARD SOCIETY. *Problems of Parliamentary Government in the Colonies.* A report prepared by the Hansard Society on some of the problems involved in developing parliamentary institutions in colonial territories. London: The Hansard Society, 1953.

HINDEN, RITA. *Local Government and the Colonies.* A report to the Fabian Colonial Bureau. London: Allen and Unwin, 1950.

HODGKIN, THOMAS. *Nationalism in Colonial Africa.* London: Frederick Muller, 1956. (American edition: New York University Press, 1957.)

INTERNATIONAL AFRICAN INSTITUTE. *Social Implications of Industrialization and Urbanization in Africa South of the Sahara.* Prepared under the auspices of UNESCO, Paris, 1956.

JEFFRIES, SIR CHARLES. *The Colonial Office.* The New Whitehall Series. London: Allen and Unwin, 1956.

KITCHEN, HELEN, *ed. The Press in Africa.* Washington, D. C.: Ruth Sloan Associates, Inc., 1956.

LEGUM, COLIN. *Must We Lose Africa?* London: W. H. Allen, 1954.

LEWIS, W. ARTHUR; SCOTT, MICHAEL; WIGHT, MARTIN; LEGUM, COLIN. *Attitude to Africa.* A survey of the main problems of British Africa, suggesting the lines of policy that any British government should follow in the years ahead. London: Penguin Books, 1951.

LUGARD, SIR F. D. *The Dual Mandate in Tropical Africa.* London: William Blackwood, 1922.

MACMILLAN, W. M. *Africa Emergent.* A survey of social, political, and economic trends in British Africa. London: Faber and Faber, 1938. (Revised and expanded edition: Penguin Books, 1949.)

MAIR, L. P. *Native Policies in Africa.* London: Routledge, 1936.

MAIR, L. P. *Studies in Applied Anthropology.* London School of Economics: Monographs on Social Anthropology. London: University of London, 1957.

MASON, PHILIP. *An Essay on Racial Tension.* London: Oxford University Press, for the Royal Institute of International Affairs, 1954.

OLIVER, ROLAND. *Sir Harry Johnston and The Scramble for Africa.* London: Chatto and Windus, 1957.

PADMORE, GEORGE. *Africa: Britain's Third Empire.* London: Denis Dobson, 1949.

PERHAM, MARGERY, LUGARD. *The Years of Adventure.* London: Collins, 1956.

PIM, SIR ALAN. *The Financial and Economic History of the African Tropical Territories.* Oxford: Clarendon Press, 1940.

SCHAPERA, I. *Government and Politics in Tribal Societies.* Josiah Mason Lectures, delivered at the University of Birmingham. London: Watts, 1956.

STILLMAN, CALVIN W., *ed. Africa in the Modern World.* Chicago: University of Chicago Press, 1955.

UNESCO. "African Elites", *International Social Science Bulletin,* Vol. 8, No. 3, 1956, pp. 413-98.

WIESCHHOFF, H. A. *Colonial Policies in Africa.* African Handbooks: No. 5. Philadelphia: University of Pennsylvania Press, 1944.

WIGHT, MARTIN. *The Development of the Legislative Council.* Studies in Colonial Legislatures, No. 1. London: Faber and Faber, 1946.

WIGHT, MARTIN. *British Colonial Constitutions, 1947.* Oxford: Clarendon Press, 1952.

Journals

Africa. Journal of the International African Institute. London, quarterly.
Africa South. Cape Town, quarterly.
African Abstracts. London, quarterly.
African Affairs. Journal of the Royal African Society. London, quarterly.
Africa Digest. London: The Africa Bureau, bi-monthly.
African World. London: African Publications, monthly.
The Colonial Review. The Colonial Department, Institute of Education, University of London, quarterly.
Commonwealth Survey. London: Commonwealth Relations Office, fortnightly.
Corona. Journal of H. M. Colonial Service. London: H. M. Stationery Office, monthly.
Journal of African Administration. London: Colonial Office, quarterly.
Journal of the Parliaments of the Commonwealth. London, quarterly.
The Round Table. London, quarterly.

BRITISH WEST AFRICA

APTER, DAVID E. "British West Africa: Patterns of Self-Government", *The Annals of the American Academy of Social and Political Science,* Vol. 298, March 1955, pp. 117-29.

AUSTIN, DENNIS. *West Africa and the Commonwealth.* London: Penguin Books (African Series), 1957.

BAUER, P. T. *West African Trade.* A study of competition, oligopoly and monopoly in a changing economy. Cambridge: The University Press, 1954.

BROWN, PAULA. "Patterns of Authority in West Africa", *Africa,* Vol. 21, No. 4, October 1954, pp. 261-78.

CARY, JOYCE. *Britain and West Africa.* London: Longmans, Green, 1946.

CHRISTENSEN, J. B. "African Political Systems: Indirect Rule and Democratic Processes", *Phylon,* Vol. 15, 1954, pp. 69-83.

CHURCH, R. J. HARRISON. *West Africa: A Study of the Environment and of Man's Use of it.* London: Longmans, Green, 1957.

DAVIDSON, BASIL, and ADAMOLA, ADENEKAN, *ed. The New West Africa: Problems of Independence.* London: Allen and Unwin, 1953.

DEGRAFT-JOHNSON, J. C. *African Glory: The Story of Vanished Negro Civilizations.* London: Watts, 1954.

FAGE, J. D. *An Introduction to the History of West Africa.* Cambridge: The University Press, 1955.

FORD, DARYLL. "Conditions of Social Development in West Africa", *Civilisations,* Vol. 3, No. 4, 1953, pp. 471-89.

GARIGUE, PHILIP. "Changing Political Leadership in West Africa", *Africa,* Vol. 24, No. 3, July 1954, pp. 220-32.

HILLIARD, F. H. *A Short History of Education in British West Africa.* Edinburgh: Nelson, 1957.

KEITH-LUCAS, B. "Electoral Procedure in Africa", *Zaïre,* Vol. 11, No. 5, May 1957, pp. 474-84.

KINGSLEY, MARY. *West African Studies.* London: Macmillan, 1899.
LITTLE, K. "The Study of 'Social Change' in British West Africa", *Africa,* Vol. 23, No. 4, October 1953, pp. 274-84.
LITTLE, KENNETH. "The Role of Voluntary Associations in West African Urbanization", *American Anthropologist,* Vol. 59, No. 4, August 1957, pp. 579-96.
MEEK, C. K., MACMILLAN, W. M., and HUSSEY, E. R. J. *Europe and West Africa: Some Problems and Adjustments.* University of London: Heath Clark Lectures, 1939. London: Oxford University Press, 1940.
NICHOLSON, MARJORIE. *West African Ferment.* Fabian Colonial Bureau Pamphlet, Research Series No. 140, July 1950.
PARRINDER, GEOFFREY. *West African Religion.* Illustrated from the beliefs and practices of the Yoruba, Ewe, Akan, and kindred peoples. London: Epworth Press, 1949.
PEDLER, F. J. *West Africa.* Home Study Books. London: Methuen, 1951.
PEDLER, F. J. *Economic Geography of West Africa.* London: Longmans, Green, 1955.
Report of the Commission on Higher Education in West Africa. Cmd. 6655. London: H.M.S.O., 1945.
TRIMINGHAM, J. S. *The Christian Church and Islam in West Africa.* London: S.C.M. Press, 1955.
WRAITH, RONALD E. "Training for Local Government in West Africa", *Journal of African Administration,* Vol. 3, October 1951.
WRAITH, RONALD E. *Local Government.* London: Penguin Books (West African Series), 1953.

Periodicals

West Africa. London, weekly.
West African Review. Liverpool, monthly.

GHANA

Of the books that have been written on Ghana, five are of special value to students interested in a sociological, historical, and constitutional background to political developments. The first, David Apter, *Gold Coast in Transition,* is an effort to deal with both tribal and colonial elements in Gold Coast society leading to the development of a mass nationalist movement. Of the studies listed here, it remains the most up-to-date. It also deals with the use of a specific form of comparative analysis useful for studies of this kind.

Capturing some of the flavor of nationalism itself, George Padmore, in his book *The Gold Coast Revolution,* gives an adequate account of the political development of the Gold Coast. The most interesting aspect of the volume, however, is the treatment of events in the colonial context through the eyes of an observer who has been close to Nkrumah and nationalism in Africa. Some of Padmore's views are also Nkrumah's views and leaders inside the CPP remain in touch with Padmore.

W. Ward, *A History of the Gold Coast* is the most important history since Claridge. It is a partly "blood and thunder" account of the events, political, social, and economic, up until the 1946 constitution of the Gold Coast. It provides the most useful and readily available account of the formation of the Ashanti nation, the establishment of British rule, and the formation of the moderate nationalist elites in the Gold Coast. It is, of course, out of date with respect to the dramatic changes in social and political life which have occurred since 1949.

Although Martin Wight did not, himself, have first hand experience of the Gold Coast, his volume, *The Gold Coast Legislative Council,* is an admirable study of politics during the inter-war period. From a legal and historical point of view, the account of the Legislative Council from 1925 until its transformation in 1946 provides the only adequate account of government and politics in that period of Gold Coast history.

A fifth volume is worthy of special note. F. M. Bourret, *The Gold Coast,* is a valuable alternative to Padmore's book. Bourret, who worked from sources she was able to obtain from Ghana and elsewhere, has written a very useful account of the political and economic changes in Ghana up until the constitutional change of 1950 (which provided a high degree of internal self government). Of particular use is a discussion of the relationship between economic policy and political policy pursued by the British and Gold Coast governments.

Of recent articles, the most significant effort to recapitulate the recent political history and current problems of Ghana is to be found in H. V. Wiseman's three articles in *Parliamentary Affairs.* These are sober and straight-forward accounts from the point of view of a political scientist. Of special interest, as well, is R. E. Wraith's discussion of the "second-chamber" issue in *Parliamentary Affairs.* This issue, and the related one of a unitary versus a federal constitution, is of particular pertinence in Africa where conditions of tribal unity and integrity must be balanced against the requirements of a national society.

Without a doubt, much of the flavor of recent events and the views of the CPP Government is most effectively brought out by Kwame Nkrumah himself in his *Autobiography.* This history of the man, not only in the heave and pull of Gold Coast nationalism, but also in the more formative years spent in the United States, go a long way in explaining the character of the political movement he helped to shape, and in helping the student to evaluate what kind of a man he is. The account does gloss over some material, such as his work on the West African Secretariat, but as events go today, it is the most important book on Ghana.

A. Government and Politics

1. Official Publications

a. Great Britain

Gold Coast Colony and Ashanti (Legislative Council) Order in Council, 1946. Statutory Rules and Orders, no. 353.

Report of the Commission of Enquiry into Disturbances in the Gold Coast, 1948. Col. 231. London: H.M.S.O., 1948.

Statement of His Majesty's Government on the Report of the Commission of Enquiry into Disturbances in the Gold Coast, 1948. Col. 232. London: H.M.S.O., 1948.

Report to His Excellency the Governor by the Committee on Constitutional Reform. (J. H. Coussey, Chairman.) Col. 248. London: H.M.S.O., 1949.

Statement by His Majesty's Government on the Report of the Committee on

Constitutional Reform. Despatch of 14th October, 1949. London: H.M.S.O., 1949.

The Gold Coast (Constitution) Order in Council, 1950. Statutory Instruments 1950, no. 2094.

The Gold Coast Constitutional Amendment No. 2, Order in Council, 1952. Statutory Instruments 1952, no. 1039.

Despatches on the Gold Coast Government's Proposals for Constitutional Reform, exchanged between the Secretary of State for the Colonies and H. E. the Governor, 24th August 1953 to 15th April 1954. Col. 302. London: H.M.S.O., 1954.

The Gold Coast (Constitution) Order in Council, 1954. Statutory Instruments 1954, no. 551.

Ghana Independence Act, 1957. 5 & 6 Eliz. 2, c.6.

b. Gold Coast

Atlas of the Gold Coast. Published by the Survey Department. Accra: Government Printer, 1949.

Report by the Select Committee on Local Government (Colony). (A. J. Loveridge, Chairman.) Accra: Government Printer, 1951.

Report of the Commission on Native Courts. (K. A. Korsah, Chairman.) Accra: Government Printer, 1951.

Regional Administrations: Report of the Commissioner (Sir Sydney Phillipson). Accra: Government Printer, 1951.

Local Government Reform in Outline. Being a summary of the three reports on local government reform and of the related proposals concerning regional administration. Accra: Government Printer, 1951.

Accelerated Development Plan for Education. Accra: Government Printer, 1951.

Local Government Ordinance of 1951. Supplement to the Gold Coast Gazette, No. 16, Jan. 16, 1952. Accra: Government Printer.

Report of the Commission of Enquiry into Wenchi Affairs. Accra: Government Printer, 1952.

The Government's Proposals for Constitutional Reform. Accra: Government Printer, 1953.

Report of the Commission of Enquiry into Representational and Electoral Reform. Sessional Paper No. 1 of 1953. Accra: Government Printer, 1954.

Report of the Select Committee on Federal System of Government and Second Chamber for the Gold Coast. Accra: Government Printer, 1955.

Report of the Constitutional Adviser (F. C. Bourne). Accra: Government Printer, 1955.

Constitutional Proposals for Gold Coast Independence and Statement on the Report of the Achimota Conference. Accra: Government Printer, 1956.

c. Ghana

Ghana Nationality and Citizenship Act. No. 1 of 1957.

Report of the Commission on Local Government Reform. (Greenwood Report.) Accra: Government Printer, 1957.

White Paper on National Workers Brigades. Accra: Government Printer, 1957.

Ghana's Policy at Home and Abroad. Information Office, Embassy of Ghana, Washington, D. C., 1957.

2. *Unofficial Publications*

a. Books

APTER, DAVID E. *The Gold Coast in Transition.* Princeton, New Jersey: Princeton University Press, 1955.

BOURRET, F. M. *The Gold Coast.* London: Oxford University Press, second edition, 1952.

CLARIDGE, W. W. *A History of the Gold Coast and Ashanti.* London: John Murray, 1915.

NKRUMAH, KWAME. *The Autobiography of Kwame Nkrumah.* Edinburgh: Nelson, 1957.

PADMORE, GEORGE. *The Gold Coast Revolution.* London: Denis Dobson, 1953.

REINDORF, CARL CHRISTIAN. *History of the Gold Coast and Asante.* Basel: Basel Book Mission, second edition, 1950.

TIMOTHY, BANKOLE. *Kwame Nkrumah.* London: Allen and Unwin, 1955.

WARD, W. E. F. *A History of the Gold Coast.* London: Allen and Unwin, 1948.

WIGHT, MARTIN. *The Gold Coast Legislative Council.* Studies in Colonial Legislatures, No. 2. London: Faber and Faber, 1947.

WRIGHT, RICHARD. *Black Power.* New York: Harper, 1954.

b. Articles and pamphlets

AMANOO, J. G. "The Position of Chiefs in Gold Coast Society", *African World,* March 1954.

APTER, DAVID E. "Political Democracy in the Gold Coast", in Calvin W. Stillman, *ed. Africa and the Modern World.* Chicago: University of Chicago Press, 1955.

APTER, DAVID E. "The Development of Ghana Nationalism", *United Asia,* Vol. 9, No. 1, February 1957, pp. 23-30.

AUSTIN, D. G. "Constitutional Development of Ghana", *United Asia,* Vol. 9, No. 1, February 1957, pp. 84-90.

BENNETT, GEORGE. "The Gold Coast General Election", *Parliamentary Affairs,* Vol. 7, No. 3, Summer 1954, pp. 430-9.

BRIGGS, ASA. "Nationalism in the Gold Coast", *Fortnightly,* n.s. 1023, 1024, March, April 1952, pp. 152-7, 231-6.

BUSIA, K. A. "The Prospects of Parliamentary Democracy in the Gold Coast", *Parliamentary Affairs,* Vol. 5, No. 4, Autumn 1952, pp. 438-44.

BUSIA, K. A. "The Gold Coast and Nigeria on the Road to Self Government", in C. Grove Haines, *ed. Africa Today.* Baltimore: Johns Hopkins, 1955.

CARTWRIGHT, MARGUERITE. "The Ghana Elections of 1956", *United Asia,* Vol. 9, No. 1, February 1957, pp. 71-9.

CHRISTENSEN, J. B. "Problems of a Society in Transition", *United Asia,* Vol. 9, No. 1, February 1957, pp. 15-22.

COLEMAN, J. S. "Togoland", *International Conciliation,* No. 509, September 1956, pp. 1-91.

CURTIN, PHILIP D. "The Gold Coast: Five Years After", *Current History,* Vol. 30, No. 177, May 1956, pp. 293-8.

DANQUAH, J. B. "Akan Claims to Origin from Ghana", *West African Review,* Vol. 26, Nos. 338, 339, November, December 1955, pp. 968-70, 1107-11.

DAVIES, S. G. "The Growth of Law in the Gold Coast", *Universitas* (Accra), Vol. 2, No. 1, December 1955, pp. 4-6. (Reprint: *Journal of African Administration,* Vol. 9, No. 2, April 1957, pp. 88-92.)

DAVIDSON, BASIL. "Historical Inheritance of Ghana", *United Asia,* Vol. 9, No. 1, February 1957, pp. 10-14.

DAVISON, R. B. "The Challenge of Ghana", *Political Quarterly,* Vol. 28, No. 3, July-September 1957, pp. 271-84.

DRAKE, ST.CLAIR. "Prospects for Democracy in the Gold Coast", *The Annals of the American Academy of Social and Political Science,* Vol. 306, July 1956, pp. 78-87.

HANNIGAN, A. ST.J. J. "Local Government in the Gold Coast", *Journal of African Administration,* Vol. 7, No. 3, July 1955, pp. 116-23.

HODGKIN, THOMAS. *Freedom for the Gold Coast?* Africa and the Future Series. London: Union of Democratic Control, 1951.

HODGKIN, THOMAS. "Ghana in the African Setting", *United Asia,* Vol. 9, No. 1, February 1957, pp. 4-9.

JONES-QUARTEY, K. A. B. "Press and Nationalism in Ghana", *United Asia,* Vol. 9, No. 1, February 1957, pp. 55-60.

LAWSON, J. S. "Operation 'Elections': The Steps Taken to Prepare the People of the Gold Coast for the Exercise of the Franchise", *Parliamentary Affairs,* Vol. 4, No. 3, 1951, pp. 332-40.

MAUNY, R. A. "The Question of Ghana", *Africa,* Vol. 24, No. 3, July 1954, pp. 200-13.

MEYEROWITZ, EVA. "A Note on the Origin of Ghana", *African Affairs,* Vol. 51, No. 205, October 1952, pp. 319-23.

PADMORE, GEORGE. "Pan-Africanism and Ghana", *United Asia,* Vol. 9, No. 1, February 1957, pp. 50-4.

PETERS, W. "Tradition and Change in the Saltpond Sub-District of the Gold Coast Colony", *Journal of African Administration,* Vol. 6, No. 1, January 1954, pp. 5-11.

"POLARIS". "The N. T.s in Gold Coast Politics", *West Africa.*
1. "The Gap between North and South", 8 May 1954, p. 419;
5. "Conservatism and Stability", 5 June 1954, p. 509.

PRICE, J. H. *The Gold Coast Election.* West African Affairs (Pub.) London, n.d.

RUSSELL, A. C., and others. "The Gold Coast General Election", *Journal of African Administration,* Vol. 3, No. 2, April 1951, pp. 65-77.

WISEMAN, H. V. "The Gold Coast: From Executive Council to Responsible Cabinet", Part I, *Parliamentary Affairs,* Vol. 10, No. 1, Winter 1956-7, pp. 27-35. "The Gold Coast: The Transition to Self Government", Part II, *Parliamentary Affairs,* Vol. 10, No. 2, Summer 1957, pp. 195-203. "The Gold Coast (Ghana): Ministers and Officials", Part III, *Parliamentary Affairs,* Vol. 10, No. 3, Summer 1957, pp. 333-43.

WRAITH, R. E. "The 'Second Chamber Question' in the Gold Coast", *Parliamentary Affairs,* Vol. 7, No. 4, Autumn 1954, pp. 393-401.

WRAITH, R. E. "Islam in the Gold Coast", *West Africa,* December 18, 25, 1954, pp. 1188, 1203.

c. Political pamphlets

BUSIA, K. A. *Judge for Yourself.* Accra: The West African Graphic, 1956.

CODJOE, DR. THOMAS A. *The Hopeless Government.* Accra: Kushara Press, 1957.

COMMITTEE ON YOUTH ORGANIZATION. *The Ghana Youth Manifesto.* Kumasi: Abura Press, 1949.

Convention Peoples Party. *Operation 104*. London: The National Labour Press, 1956.

Convention Peoples Party. *Manifesto of the Convention Peoples Party*. Accra: West African Graphic, 1956.

Convention Peoples Party. *Convention Peoples Party Songs and Hymns*. Accra: West African Graphic, n.d.

Convention Peoples Party. *Togoland and Gold Coast*. Accra: West African Graphic, n.d.

Danquah, Dr. J. B. *Self Help and Expansion*. Gold Coast Youth Conference. Achimota: Achimota Press, 1943.

Danquah, Dr. J. B. *The Doyen Speaks*. Accra: West African Graphic, 1957.

Danquah, Moses. *Political Agitation in the Gold Coast*. Accra: United Gold Coast Convention, 1950.

Equapoo, Mrs. Rose Y. *First Justice Then Peace*. Accra: West African Graphic, 1952.

Ghana Congress Party. *Manifesto of the Ghana Congress Party*. Accra: West African Graphic, 1956.

Gold Coast Youth Conference. *First Steps Toward a National Fund*. Achimota: Achimota Press, 1938.

National Liberation Movement. *Proposals for a Federal Constitution for an Independent Gold Coast and Togoland*. Movements and Parties other than Convention Peoples Party. Kumasi: Abura Printing Works, 1956.

Nkrumah, Kwame. *The New Stage (Convention Peoples Party Versus Imperialism)*. Convention Peoples Party. Accra: Nyaniba Press, 1951.

Trades Union Congress. *Constitution, Rules and Standing Orders*. (mimeo.) Accra, 1956.

United Gold Coast Convention. *The Country's Demand*. Accra: West African Graphic, 1950.

United Gold Coast Convention. *Ten Point Programme and Re-Affirmation of Policy*. National Consultative Conference. Accra: West African Graphic, 1950.

United Gold Coast Convention. *The 'P' Plan*. United Gold Coast Convention. Accra: Iona Press, 1952.

B. Anthropology

1. Northern Territories

Cardinall, A. W. *The Natives of the Northern Territories of the Gold Coast*. London: Routledge, 1925.

Fortes, Meyer. *The Dynamics of Clanship among the Tallensi*. London: Oxford University Press, for the International African Institute, 1945.

Fortes, Meyer. *The Web of Kinship among the Tallensi*. London: Oxford University Press, for the International African Institute, 1949.

Manoukian, Madeline. *Tribes of the Northern Territories of the Gold Coast*. Ethnographic Survey of Africa: Western Africa, Part V. London: International African Institute, 1952.

Rattray, R. S. *The Tribes of the Ashanti Hinterland*. Oxford: Clarendon Press, 1952.

Tait, David. "The Political System of the Konkomba", *Africa*, Vol. 23, No. 3, July 1953, pp. 213-23.

2. *Akan*

Beckett, W. H. *Akokoaso: A Survey of a Gold Coast Village.* London School of Economics: Monographs on Social Anthropology, No. 10. London, 1944.

Busia, K. A. *The Position of the Chief in the Modern Political System of Ashanti.* London: Oxford University Press, for the International African Institute, 1951.

Busia, K. A. "The Ashanti", in Daryll Forde, *ed. African Worlds.* London: Oxford University Press, for the International African Institute, 1954.

Christensen, J. B. *Double Descent Among the Fanti.* Human Relations Area Files, New Haven, 1954.

Danquah, J. B. *Akan Laws and Customs and the Akim Abuakwa Constitution.* London: Routledge, 1928.

Field, Margaret Joyce. *Akim-Kotoku, An Oman of the Gold Coast.* Accra: Government Printer, 1948.

Fortes, Meyer. "The Ashanti Social Survey", *Human Problems in British Central Africa,* No. 6, 1945, pp. 1-36.

Manoukian, Madeline. *Akan and Ga-Adangme Peoples of the Gold Coast.* Ethnographic Survey of Africa: Western Africa, Part I. London: Oxford University Press, for the International African Institute, 1950.

Meyerowitz, Eva. *The Sacred State of the Akan.* London: Faber and Faber, 1951.

Meyerowitz, Eva. *Akan Traditions of Origin.* London: Faber and Faber, 1952.

Rattray, R. S. *Ashanti.* Oxford: Clarendon Press, 1923.

Rattray, R. S. *Ashanti Law and Constitution.* Oxford: Clarendon Press, 1929.

3. *Ga and Ewe*

Field, Margaret Joyce. *Social Organization of the Ga People.* London: Crown Agents, 1940.

Manoukian, Madeline. *The Ewe-Speaking People of Togoland and the Gold Coast.* Ethnographic Survey of Africa: Western Africa, Part VI. London: International African Institute, 1952.

C. *Economics*

Apter, David E. "Some Economic Factors in the Political Development of the Gold Coast", *Journal of Economic History,* Vol. 14, No. 4, October 1954, pp. 409-27.

Busia, K. A. *Report on a Social Survey of Sekondi-Takoradi.* London: Crown Agents, for the Gold Coast Government, 1950.

Lewis, W. A. *Report on Industrialization and the Gold Coast.* Accra: Government Printer, 1953.

Seers, Dudley, and Ross, C. R. *Report on Financial and Physical Problems of Development in the Gold Coast.* Accra: Office of the Government Statistician (mimeograph), 1952.

Newspapers

The Ashanti Pioneer. (National Liberation Movement.) Kumasi, daily.

The Daily Graphic. (Independent.) Accra, daily.

The Ghana Evening News. (Convention Peoples Party.) Accra, daily.

Other Periodicals

Proceedings of the Gold Coast and Togoland Historical Society. Accra.
Ghana Public Servant. Published by the Ghana Civil Service, Accra.
Ghana Today. Published by the Information Section, Ghana Office, London.
The Ghana Worker. Published by the Ghana Trades Union Congress, Accra.
Universitas. University College of Ghana.

NIGERIA

There are few general studies of Nigerian history and political development. Sir Alan Burns *History of Nigeria,* recently revised, is a standard account from the official British point of view. There are several studies of British West Africa, the most useful short work being J. D. Fage, *An Introduction to the History of West Africa.* C. R. Niven, *Nigeria: Outline of a Colony,* is also an introductory work. The only study of Nigerian government from the center is that by Joan Wheare, *The Nigerian Legislative Council;* this account terminates with the 1946 Constitution. For the student of colonial government, the chief interest in Nigeria has always been in the application of the principles of Indirect Rule, and this has led to a concentration of interest in regional and local government. Sir F. D. Lugard, *The Dual Mandate in British Tropical Africa* is an exposition of this policy by its founder. Volume III of Lord Hailey, *Native Administration in the British African Territories* describes the system in operation; a less official and more thorough account of its working is given by M. Perham, *Native Administration in Nigeria.* An early criticism of the system is provided in W. R. Crocker, *Nigeria: A Critique of British Colonial Administration;* an account of its working in relation to modern ideas and developments in local government is given by an African District Officer, N. U. Akpan, *Epitaph to Indirect Rule.* There are numerous articles on recent developments in local government in Nigeria, mostly in the *Journal of African Administration* and *West Africa;* those by P. C. Lloyd are the most valuable. P. J. Harris, *Local Government in Southern Nigeria* gives a general account of these developments, with the local government laws of the two southern regions as an appendix; I. D. Cameron and B. K. Cooper, *The West African Councillor,* is a textbook of local government practice for councillors.

For recent nationalist movements and constitutional developments there is little secondary material. J. S. Coleman, *Nationalism in Nigeria,* a Ph.D. thesis for Harvard University, now being published by the University of California Press, is the only thorough study. O. Awolowo, *Path to Nigerian Freedom,* is an early statement of nationalist aims by the leader of the Action Group. Ruth Perry, *A Preliminary Bibliography of the Literature of Nationalism in Nigeria* indicates most of the material available, but most of these are pamphlets printed in Nigeria. The Weekly, *West Africa* is sympathetic to African views and contains articles, reports of speeches, and letters expressing African political opinion. The official reports of the several constitutional conferences are presently the only complete source for constitutional developments. The published Debates of the Nigerian legislatures record the opinions expressed there.

The varied nature of the African groups in Nigeria has provided a wide variety of anthropological works, and studies of indigenous political systems. S. F. Nadel, *A Black Byzantium* is particularly valuable in presenting insights into the functioning of Nupe society, and C. K. Meek, *Law and Authority in a Nigerian Tribe,* discusses the realities of political authority in Ibo society. T. O. Elias, in *Nigerian Land Law and Custom* and *The Nature of African Customary Law* has provided information on the indigenous legal systems of Nigeria, and their development as vehicles for modern administration, as seen from the viewpoint of a British-trained African lawyer.

The report prepared by the International Bank, *The Economic Development of Nigeria,* is the most useful handbook on economic conditions in Nigeria, while the U. S. Department of Commerce publication, *Investment in Nigeria,* also provides a valuable summary on economic conditions. The two volumes of *The Economics of a Tropical Dependency,* edited by M. Perham, are scholarly studies of both indigenous and modern developments up to the end of World War II.

A. Government and Politics

1. Official Publications

a. United Nations

Trusteeship Council. *United Nations Visiting Mission to Trust Territories in West Africa, 1952:* Report on the Cameroons under United Kingdom administration. T/1042. New York, 1953.

b. Great Britain

Proposals for the Revision of the Constitution of Nigeria. Cmd. 6599. London: H.M.S.O., 1945.

Report by the Conference on the Nigerian Constitution, held in London in July and August, 1953. Cmd. 8934. London: H.M.S.O., 1953.

Nigeria Protectorate. The Nigeria (Constitution) (amendment) Order in Council, 1953. Statutory Instruments 1953, no. 740.

The Nigeria (Constitution) (amendment) Order in Council, 1953. Statutory Instruments 1953, no. 1566.

Report by the Resumed Conference on the Nigerian Constitution, held in Lagos in January and February, 1954. Cmd. 9059. London: H.M.S.O., 1954.

Report by the Nigeria Constitutional Conference. (May 23-June 26, 1957.) Cmnd. 207. London: H.M.S.O., 1957.

c. Nigeria

Cameron, Sir Donald. *The Principles of Native Administration and their Application.* Lagos: Government Printer, 1934.

Bourdillon, Sir Bernard. *Memorandum on the Future Political Development of Nigeria.* Lagos: Government Printer, 1939.

Phillipson, M. *Administrative and Financial Procedure under the New Constitution:* Financial relations between the government of Nigeria and the native administrations. Lagos: Government Printer, 1947.

Apportionment of Duties between the Government of Nigeria and Native Administration: Statement of Policy. Lagos: Government Printer, 1947.

Report of a Select Committtee of the Eastern Region House of Assembly set up to review the existing system of Local Government in the Eastern Provinces. Lagos: Government Printer, 1948.

Review of the Constitution: Regional Recommendations. Lagos: Government Printer, 1949.

Proceedings of the General Conference on Review of the Constitution, January 1950. Lagos: Government Printer, 1950.

Report of the Drafting Committtee of the Constitution. Lagos: Government Printer, 1950.

Review of the Constitution of Nigeria. Dispatch from the Secretary of State dated July 15, 1950. Lagos: Government Printer, 1950.

Handbook of Constitutional Instruments. Lagos: Government Printer, 1950.

Local Government in the Western Provinces of Nigeria. Ibadan: Government Printer, 1951.

The Nigeria (Constitution) Order in Council, 1951. Statutory Instruments 1951, no. 1172.

Report on the Kano Disturbances, 16, 17, 18, and 19 May, 1953. Kaduna: Government Printer, 1953.

FENTON, J. S. *Report on a Visit to Nigeria, and on the Application of the Principles of Native Administration to Sierra Leone.* Sessional Paper no. 3. Freetown: Government Printer, 1953.

MADDOCKS, K. P., and POTT, D. A. *Report on Local Government in the Northern Provinces of Nigeria.* Kaduna: Government Printer, 1953.

POTT, D. A. *Progress Report on Local Government in the Northern Region of Nigeria.* Kaduna: Government Printer, 1953.

EASTERN REGION. *Policy for Local Government and Co-operative Societies.* Sessional Paper no. 4. Enugu: Government Printer, 1953.

Nigeria (Constitution) Order in Council, 1954. Statutory Instruments, no. 1146.

Nigeria (Offices of Governor-General and Governors) Order in Council, 1954. Statutory Instruments, no. 1147.

The Nigeria Handbook. London: Crown Agents, on behalf of the Government of Nigeria, second edition, 1954.

2. *Unofficial Publications*

a. Books

AKPAN, NTIEYONG U. *Epitaph to Indirect Rule: A Discourse on Local Government in Africa.* London: Cassell, 1956.

AWOLOWO, OBAFEMI. *Path to Nigerian Freedom.* London: Faber and Faber, 1947.

BURNS, SIR ALAN. *History of Nigeria.* London: Allen and Unwin, revised edition, 1956.

CAMERON, I. D. and COOPER, B. K. *The West African Councillor.* London: Oxford University Press, 1954.

COLEMAN, J. S. *Nigeria: Background to Nationalism.* Berkeley and Los Angeles: University of California Press (forthcoming Fall, 1958).

CROCKER, W. R. *Nigeria: A Critique of British Colonial Administration.* London: Allen and Unwin, 1936.

DIKE, K. ONWUKA. *Trade and Politics in the Niger Delta, 1830-1885.* An introduction to the economic and political history of Nigeria. Oxford: Clarendon Press, 1956.

ELIAS, T. OLAWALE. *Nigerian Land Law and Custom.* London: Routledge and Kegan Paul, second edition, 1953.

HARRIS, P. J. *Local Government in Southern Nigeria.* Cambridge: University Press, 1957.

LUGARD, LADY (FLORA SHAW). *A Tropical Dependency.* London: Nisbet and Company, 1905.

MEEK, C. K. *Law and Authority in a Nigerian Tribe: A Study in Indirect Rule.* London: Oxford University Press, 1937.

NIVEN, C. R. *Nigeria: Outline of a Colony.* London: Nelson, 1946.

PERHAM, MARGERY. *Native Administration in Nigeria.* London: Oxford University Press, 1937.

WHEARE, JOAN. *The Nigerian Legislative Council.* Studies in Colonial Legislatures, No. 4. London: Faber and Faber, 1950.

b. Articles and pamphlets.

ABUBAKAR, IMAM, MALAM. "Nigerian Constitutional Proposals", *African Affairs,* Vol. 45, No. 178, January 1946, pp. 22-7.

AKPAN, NTIEYONG U. "Chieftaincy in Eastern Nigeria", *Journal of African Administration,* Vol. 9, No. 3, July 1957, pp. 120-4.

ALUKO, S. A. *The Problems of Self-Government for Nigeria: A Critical Analysis.* Ilfracombe, Devon: Arthur H. Stockwell, 1955.

BROWN, R. E. "Local Government in the West Region of Nigeria 1950-1955", *Journal of African Administration,* Vol. 7, No. 4, October 1955, pp. 180-8.

COLEMAN, J. S. "The Role of Tribal Associations in Nigeria", *Conference Proceedings,* West African Institute of Social and Economic Research, Ibadan, April 1952.

HAFTER, R. P. "Nigeria on the Road to Autonomy", *Swiss Review of World Affairs,* Vol. 4, September 1954, pp. 14-18.

JONES, G. I. *Report of the Position, Status and Influence of Chiefs and Natural Rulers in the Eastern Region of Nigeria.* Enugu: Government Printer, Eastern Region, 1957.

LIVINGSTON BOOTH, J. D. "Oiling the Wheels of Local Government in Eastern Nigeria", *Journal of African Administration,* Vol. 7, No. 2, April 1955, pp. 55-64.

LLOYD, P. C. "Kings, Chiefs and Local Government", *West Africa,* January 31, February 7, 1953, pp. 79, 103.

LLOYD, P. C. "The Integration of the New Economic Classes into Local Government in Western Nigeria", *African Affairs,* Vol. 52, No. 209, October 1953, pp. 327-34.

LLOYD, P. C. "Action Group and Local Government", *West Africa,* November 7, 1953, p. 1039.

LLOYD, P. C. "The Development of Political Parties in Western Nigeria", *American Political Science Review,* Vol. 49, No. 3, September 1955, pp. 693-707.

(MAIR, L. P.) "Nigeria under the Macpherson Constitution", *World Today,* Vol. 9, No. 1, January 1953, pp. 12-21.

MORTON-WILLIAMS, P. "Some Yoruba Kingdoms under Modern Conditions", *Journal of African Administration,* Vol. 7, No. 4, October 1955, pp. 174-9.

OTTENBERG, S. "Improvement Associations among the Afikpo Ibo", *Africa,* Vol. 25, No. 1, January 1955, pp. 1-28.

"Provincial Authorities in the Northern Region of Nigeria. A Note on the Report of the 'Hudson' Commission", *Journal of African Administration,* Vol. 9, No. 3, July 1957, pp. 139-44.

TUGBIYELE, AKANDE. *The Emergence of Nationalism and Federalism in Nigeria.* P.O. Box 7, Agbor, Nigeria, 1956.

B. Anthropology

BASCOM, W. "Urbanization among the Yoruba", *American Journal of Sociology*, Vol. 60, No. 5, March, 1955, pp. 446-54.

BOHANNAN, PAUL. *Justice and Judgement Among the Tiv*. London: Oxford University Press, for the International African Institute, 1957.

BOHANNAN, LAURA, and BOHANNAN, PAUL. *The Tiv of Central Nigeria*. Ethnographic Survey of Africa: Western Africa, Part VIII. London: International African Institute, 1953.

FORDE, DARYLL. "Government in Umor: a study of social change and problems of indirect rule in a Nigerian village community", *Africa*, Vol. 12, No. 2, April 1939, pp. 129-61.

FORDE, DARYLL, and JONES, G. I. *The Ibo and Ibibio Speaking Peoples of South-Eastern Nigeria*. Ethnographic Survey of Africa: Western Africa, Part III. London: Oxford University Press, for the International African Institute, 1950.

FORDE, DARYLL, and others. *Peoples of the Niger-Benue Confluence*. Ethnographic Survey of Africa: Western Africa, Part X. London: International African Institute, 1955.

FORDE, DARYLL. *The Yoruba-Speaking Peoples of South-Western Nigeria*. Ethnographic Survey of Africa: Western Africa, Part IV. London: International African Institute, 1951.

GREEN, M. M. *Ibo Village Affairs:* chiefly with reference to the village of Umueko Agbaha. London: Sidgewick and Jackson, 1948.

GUNN, HAROLD D. *Peoples of the Plateau Area of Northern Nigeria*. Ethnographic Survey of Africa: Western Africa, Part VII. London: International African Institute, 1953.

LLOYD, P. C. "The Traditional Political System of the Yoruba", *Southwestern Journal of Anthropology*, Vol. 10, No. 4, Winter 1954, pp. 366-84.

MCCULLOCH, MERRAN; LITTLEWOOD, MARGARET; and DUGAST, I. *Peoples of the Central Cameroons (Tikar, Bamum, Bamileke, Banen, Bafia and Balom)*. Ethnographic Survey of Africa: Western Africa, Part IX. London: International African Institute, 1954.

MEEK, C. K. *The Northern Tribes of Nigeria:* an ethnographical account of the Northern Provinces of Nigeria, together with a report on the 1921 decennial census. 2 vols. London: Oxford University Press, 1925.

MEEK, C. K. *Tribal Studies in Northern Nigeria*. 2 vols. London: Kegan Paul, 1931.

NADEL, S. F. *A Black Byzantium: the Kingdom of the Nupe in Nigeria*. London: Oxford University Press, for the International African Institute, 1942.

C. Economics

BOWER, P. A., and others. *Mining, Commerce and Finance in Nigeria*. Part II of M. Perham, *ed. The Economics of a Tropical Dependency*. London: Faber and Faber, for Nuffield College, 1948.

BUCHANAN, K. M., and PUGH, J. C. *Land and People in Nigeria*. London: University of London Press, 1955.

Development of the Western Region of Nigeria, 1955-1960. Sessional Paper No. 4. Western Region, Nigeria: Government Printer, 1955.

FORDE, DARYLL, and SCOTT, RICHENDA. *The Native Economies of Nigeria.* Part I of M. Perham, *ed. The Economics of a Tropical Dependency.* London: Faber and Faber, for Nuffield College, 1946.

GALLETTI, R., and others. *Nigerian Cocoa Farmers.* London: Oxford University Press, for the Nigerian Cocoa Marketing Board, 1956.

Handbook of Commerce and Industry in Nigeria. Lagos: Federal Department of Commerce and Industries, 1957.

INTERNATIONAL BANK FOR RECONSTRUCTION AND DEVELOPMENT. *The Economic Development of Nigeria.* Report of a mission organized . . . at the request of the Governments of Nigeria and the United Kingdom. Lagos: Federal Government Printer, 1954.

Investment in Nigeria. Basic Information for United States Businessmen. Washington, D. C.: U. S. Department of Commerce, 1957.

SMITH, M. G. *The Economy of Hausa Communities of Zaria.* Colonial Research Studies, No. 16. London: H.M.S.O., 1955.

Newspapers

The Daily Times. (Independent). Lagos, daily.

West African Pilot. (National Council of Nigeria and the Cameroons). Lagos, daily.

The Daily Service. (Action Group). Lagos, daily.

The Nigerian Tribune. (Action Group). Ibadan, daily.

Southern Nigerian Defender. (National Council of Nigeria and the Cameroons). Ibadan, daily.

Eastern Nigerian Guardian. (National Council of Nigeria and the Cameroons). Port Harcourt, daily.

Eastern States Daily Express. (United National Independence Party). Aba, daily.

Daily Comet. (Northern Elements Progressive Union). Kano, daily.

Nigerian Citizen. (Pro-Northern Peoples Congress). Zaria, weekly.

Other Periodicals

Journal of the Historical Society of Nigeria. Ibadan, quarterly.

News from Nigeria. Federal Information Service, Lagos, bi-weekly.

FEDERATION OF RHODESIA AND NYASALAND

There is no modern authoritative book on the history and political development of Central Africa. Probably the most useful historical introduction is contained in E. A. Walker, *A History of Southern Africa,* although the sections on Central Africa form only a small part of the book. Lord Hailey, *An African Survey,* describes the administration of the areas, and R. L. Buell, *The Native Problem in Africa,* indicates the developments up to 1928. Both the studies of W. K. Hancock, *Survey of British Commonwealth Affairs,* Vol. II and W. M. Macmillan, *Africa Emergent* contain valuable discussions of white settlement and native policy. The two recent scholarly works of A. J. Hanna and L. H. Gann describe the early years of settlement in Northern Rhodesia and Nyasaland; the various biographies of Cecil Rhodes, of which only the most important is listed here, give accounts of the British South Africa Company and the founding of the

Rhodesias. J. W. Davidson, *The Northern Rhodesia Legislative Council,* is the only account of political development in that area up to World War II. Other books on Central Africa are mostly journalistic surveys, or accounts written to express a point of view; J. H. Oldham, *New Hope in Africa,* pleads the case for development according to the ideals of the Capricorn Africa Society; Don Taylor, *The Rhodesian,* the recent biography of Sir Roy Welensky, gives the background to the federation controversy, and some insight into the character of the present Prime Minister.

Articles and pamphlets give the most useful assessment of modern conditions. K. Kirkwood, E. Dvorin and C. G. Rosberg have written scholarly studies of race relations and political developments since federation. Philip Mason, *An Essay on Racial Tension,* gives a general discussion of race relations. The several pamphlets listed supporting or opposing federation show the arguments used in this continuing debate.

In the absence of general secondary works, the government reports still form the basis of political studies. The numerous British Command Papers document the federation proposals, and the details of governmental amalgamation. Special mention should be made of the Tredgold Commission's report on the Southern Rhodesian franchise and the theories of representation it contains. Debates in the legislatures provide material on policies and opinions, and the periodicals *Federation of Rhodesia and Nyasaland Newsletter* and *East Africa and Rhodesia* report current political events.

The Rhodes-Livingstone Institute has fostered anthropological studies in this area, and the works of J. A. Barnes, E. Colson, Max Gluckman, and J. C. Mitchell, among others, provide material not only on the indigenous political systems, but on the nature of modern social change in African society. G. and M. Wilson, *The Analysis of Social Change,* provides a theoretical framework for the consideration of these developments. Valuable studies on the African under urban conditions have been made by the Wilsons, J. C. Mitchell and A. L. Epstein; these form a basis for the study of African political developments.

Official reports provide most of the information for economic studies. H. W. Woodruff, *Economic Conditions in the Federation of Rhodesia and Nyasaland,* discusses the economy in general while Phyllis Deane, *Colonial Social Accountings,* makes use of national income accounting to illuminate the structure of the economy. Perhaps the best economic survey is *Investment in the Federation of Rhodesia and Nyasaland,* published by the U. S. Department of Commerce. *The Monthly Digest of Statistics,* published by the Central African Statistical Office is the authoritative source for current developments.

A. *Government and Politics*

1. *Official Publications*

a. *Great Britain*

First Report of a Committee Appointed by the Secretary of State for the Colonies to consider certain questions relating to Rhodesia. Cmd. 1273. London: H.M.S.O., 1921. *Second Report . . .* Cmd. 1471. London: H.M.S.O., 1921.

Report of the Commission on Closer Union of the Dependencies in Eastern and Central Africa. Cmd. 3234. London: H.M.S.O., 1929.

Rhodesia-Nyasaland Royal Commission Report. Cmd. 5949. London: H.M.S.O., 1939.

Central African Territories: Report of Conference on Closer Association. Cmd. 8233. London: H.M.S.O., 1951.

Central African Territories: Geographical, Historical and Economic Survey. Cmd. 8234. London: H.M.S.O., 1951.

Central African Territories: Comparative Survey of Native Policy. Cmd. 8235. London: H.M.S.O., 1951.

Closer Association in Central Africa (Statement by His Majesty's Government in the United Kingdom, 21st November 1951). Cmd. 8411. London: H.M.S.O., 1951.

Southern Rhodesia, Northern Rhodesia and Nyasaland: Draft Federal Scheme (prepared by a conference in London in April and May, 1952). Cmd. 8573. London: H.M.S.O., 1952.

Southern Rhodesia, Northern Rhodesia and Nyasaland: Draft Federal Scheme. Report of the Judicial Commission. Cmd. 8671. London: H.M.S.O., 1952.

Southern Rhodesia, Northern Rhodesia and Nyasaland: Draft Federal Scheme. Report of the Fiscal Commission. Cmd. 8672. London: H.M.S.O., 1952.

Southern Rhodesia, Northern Rhodesia and Nyasaland: Draft Federal Scheme. Report of the Civil Service Preparatory Commission. Cmd. 8673. London: H.M.S.O., 1952.

Southern Rhodesia, Northern Rhodesia and Nyasaland: Report by the Conference on Federation (held in London in January, 1953). Cmd. 8753. London: H.M.S.O., 1953.

Southern Rhodesia, Northern Rhodesia and Nyasaland: The Federal Scheme (prepared by a conference held in London in January, 1953). Cmd. 8754. London: H.M.S.O., 1953.

Rhodesia and Nyasaland Federation Act. 1 & 2 Eliz. 2, c30.

Federation of Rhodesia and Nyasaland (Constitution) Order in Council, 1953. (Annex: Constitution of the Federation of Rhodesia and Nyasaland.) Statutory Instruments 1953, no. 1199.

Federation of Rhodesia and Nyasaland (Commencement) Order in Council, 1953. Statutory Instruments, 1953.

b. Rhodesia and Nyasaland

CENTRAL AFRICAN COUNCIL. *Report of the Commission on Higher Education for Africans in Central Africa.* (Sir Alexander Carr-Saunders, Chairman.) Salisbury, 1953.

Northern Rhodesia:

Report of the Commission to Inquire into the Status and Welfare of Coloured Persons in Northern Rhodesia. Lusaka: Government Printer, 1950.

Report of the Commission to Inquire into the Advancement of Africans in Industry. (A. Dalgleish, Chairman.) Lusaka: Government Printer, 1952.

Report of the Committee on African and Eurafrican Housing in Lusaka. Lusaka: Government Printer, 1953.

The Northern Rhodesia Handbook. Lusaka: Government Printer, 1953.

Advancement of Africans in the Copper Mining Industry. Report by Sir John Forster. Lusaka: Government Printer, 1954.

Report of the Committee Appointed to Investigate the Extent to which Racial Discrimination is Practised in Shops and in other similar Business Premises. (B. P. de R. O'Byrne, Chairman.) Lusaka: Government Printer, 1956.

Report of the Commission Appointed to Inquire into the Unrest in the Mining Industry in Northern Rhodesia in recent months. (Sir Patrick Branigan, Chairman.) Lusaka: Government Printer, 1956.

Report of the Committee Appointed to Examine and Recommend Ways and Means by which Africans Resident in Municipal and Township Areas should be enabled to take an appropriate part in the administration of those areas. (J. R. Brown, Chairman.) Lusaka: Government Printer, 1957.

Nyasaland:

MURRAY, S. S. *The Handbook of Nyasaland.* London: Crown Agents for the Colonies, 1932.

Southern Rhodesia:

Southern Rhodesia Constitution Letters Patent, 1923. (With amendments to date.)

Report of the Land Commission. Salisbury: Government Printer, 1925.

The Year Book of Southern Rhodesia. No. 4. Salisbury: Rhodesian Printing and Publishing Co., 1952.

What the Native Land Husbandry Act Means to the Rural African and to Southern Rhodesia. A five year plan that will revolutionise African agriculture. Salisbury: Government Printer, 1955.

Report of the Franchise Commission. (Sir Robert Tredgold, Chairman.) Salisbury: Government Printer, 1957.

Summary of Proposed New Franchise Provisions. Issued by the Southern Rhodesia Government. Salisbury: Government Printer, 1957.

2. *Unofficial Publications*

a. Books

BATE, H. MACLEAR. *Report from the Rhodesias.* London: Andrew Melrose, 1953.

DAVIDSON, J. W. *The Northern Rhodesian Legislative Council.* Studies in Colonial Legislatures, No. 3. London: Faber and Faber, 1948.

DEBENHAM, FRANK. *Nyasaland: The Land of the Lake.* London: H.M.S.O., 1955.

GANN, L. H. *The Birth of a Plural Society: Northern Rhodesia under the British South Africa Company 1894-1914.* Manchester: Manchester University Press, for the Rhodes-Livingston Institute (in press).

HANNA, A. J. *The Beginnings of Nyasaland and North-Eastern Rhodesia 1859-95.* Oxford: Clarendon Press, 1956.

JOHNSTON, SIR H. H. *British Central Africa.* London: Methuen, 1897.

KANE, NORA S. *The World's View: The Story of Southern Rhodesia.* London: Cassel, 1954.

LESSING, DORIS. *Going Home.* London: Michael Joseph, 1957.

OLDHAM, J. H. *New Hope in Africa.* London: Longmans, Green, 1955.

TAYLOR, DON. *Rainbow on the Zambezi.* London: Museum Press, 1953.

TAYLOR, DON. *The Rhodesian: The Life of Sir Roy Welensky.* London: Museum Press, 1955.

WALLIS, J. P. R. *One Man's Hand: The Story of Sir Charles Coghlan and the Liberation of Southern Rhodesia.* London: Longmans, Green, 1950.

WILLIAMS, BASIL. *Cecil Rhodes.* London: Constable, 1938.

b. Articles and pamphlets

African Affairs in Southern Rhodesia. Salisbury: Department of African Affairs, n.d. 1957 (?).

BANDA, HASTINGS R., and NKUMBULA, HARRY. *Federation in Central Africa.* London, 1949.

Central Africa and the British Parliament. Background to the Constitution Amendment Bill: 1957. London: The Africa Bureau, 1957.

CREECH JONES, A. *African Challenge: The Fallacy of Federation.* London: The Africa Bureau, 1952.

DVORIN, EUGENE P. "Central Africa's First Federal Election: Background and Issues", *Western Political Quarterly,* Vol. 7, No. 3, September 1954, pp. 369-90.

DVORIN, EUGENE P. *The Central African Federation: A Political Analysis.* University of California, Los Angeles, 1955. Unpublished Ph.D. dissertation.

EPSTEIN, A. L. *The Administration of Justice and the Urban African:* a study of urban native courts in Northern Rhodesia. Colonial Research Studies, No. 7. London: H.M.S.O., 1953.

FARQUHAR, J. H. "Political Representation of the African", *NADA,* No. 23, 1946, pp. 62-7.

HOCHSCHILD, HAROLD K. "Labor Relations in Northern Rhodesia", *The Annals of the American Academy of Political and Social Science,* Vol. 306, July 1956, pp. 43-9.

IRVINE, KEITH. "The Central African Federation", *Current History,* Vol. 30, No. 177, May 1956, pp. 285-92.

IBBOTSON, PERCY. *Report on Native Councils, Bulawayo:* Federation of African Welfare Societies in Southern Rhodesia, 1952.

KIRKWOOD, KENNETH. *The Proposed Federation of the Central African Territories.* New Africa Pamphlet No. 21. Johannesburg: The South African Institute of Race Relations, n.d. 1952 (?).

KIRKWOOD, KENNETH. "British Central Africa: Politics under Federation", *Annals of the American Academy of Political and Social Science,* Vol. 298, March 1955, pp. 130-41.

KIRKWOOD, KENNETH. "Ethnic and Cultural Pluralism in British Central Africa", INCIDI (International Institute of Differing Civilizations), *Ethnic and Cultural Pluralism in Intertropical Communities.* Report of the 30th Meeting held in Lisbon, April 1957, pp. 294-324. Brussels, 1957.

MAIR, L. P. *Native Administration in Central Nyasaland.* London: H.M.S.O., for the Colonial Office, 1952.

MASON, PHILIP. "Masters or Partners? Race Relations in the African Federation", *Foreign Affairs,* Vol. 35, No. 3, April 1957, 496-506.

MITCHELL, J. CLYDE. "The African Middle Classes in British Central Africa", INCIDI (International Institute of Differing Civilizations), *Development of a Middle Class in Tropical and Sub-Tropical Countries.* Record of the 29th Session held in London, September 1955, pp. 222-32. Brussels, 1955.

MNYANDA, B. J. *In Search of Truth: a Commentary on Certain Aspects of Southern Rhodesia's Native Policy.* Bombay: Hind Kitabs, 1954.

MTEPUKA, ELIAS M. "Central African Federation, (I) The Attack", *Africa South,* Vol. 1, No. 4, July-Sept., 1957, pp. 73-81.

Our Trust in Central Africa: A Study of the Scheme for Central African Federation. Peace Aims Pamphlet No. 56. London: National Peace Council, n.d. 1953 (?).

A Petition to Her Majesty Queen Elizabeth II against Federation made by Chiefs and Citizens of Nyasaland. With a postscript by A. Creech Jones. London: Africa Bureau, 1953.

ROSBERG, CARL G., JR. "The Federation of Rhodesia and Nyasaland: Problems of Democratic Government", *The Annals of the American Academy of Political and Social Science,* Vol. 306, July 1956, pp. 98-105.

SHEPPERTON, GEORGE. "The Politics of African Separatist Church Movements, 1892-1916", *Africa,* Vol. 24, No. 3, July 1954, pp. 233-46.

WILSON, N. H.; NYIRENDA, ABEL, HLAZO, T. J. *Federation and the African.* The Case for Federation . . . from the African viewpoint. Salisbury: Capricorn Africa Society, May 1952.

WILSON, N. H. *Central African Dilemma.* Salisbury, 1954.

B. Anthropology

BARNES, J. A. "Some Aspects of Political Development among the Fort Jameson Ngoni", *African Studies,* Vol. 7, Nos. 2-3, June-Sept. 1948, pp. 99-109.

BARNES, J. A. *Politics in a Changing Society:* a political history of the Fort Jameson Ngoni. Cape Town: Oxford University Press, for the Rhodes-Livingstone Institute, 1954.

BRELSFORD, W. V. *The Succession of the Bemba Chiefs: A Guide for District Officers.* Lusaka: Printed by the Government Printer, 1946.

BULLOCK, CHARLES. *The Mashona and the Matabele.* Cape Town: Juta, 1950.

COLSON, E. "Modern Political Organization of the Plateau Tonga", *African Studies,* Vol. 7, Nos. 2-3, June-Sept. 1948, pp. 85-98.

COLSON, ELIZABETH, and GLUCKMAN, MAX, *eds. Seven Tribes of British Central Africa.* London: Oxford University Press, for the Rhodes-Livingstone Institute, 1951.

COLSON, E. "Social Control and Vengeance in Plateau Tonga Society", *Africa,* Vol. 23, No. 3, July 1953, pp. 199-212.

CUNNISON, IAN G. *Kinship and Local Organisation of the Luapula.* Communications, No. 5. Livingstone: Rhodes-Livingstone Institute, 1950.

EPSTEIN, A. L. *Politics in an Urban African Community.* Manchester: Manchester University Press, for the Rhodes-Livingstone Institute, 1958.

GLUCKMAN, MAX. *Economy of the Central Barotse Plain.* Livingstone: Rhodes-Livingstone Institute (Papers No. 7), 1941.

GLUCKMAN, MAX; MITCHELL, J. C.; and BARNES, J. A. "The Village Headman in British Central Africa", *Africa,* Vol. 19, No. 2, April 1949, pp. 89-100.

GLUCKMAN, MAX. *The Judicial Process among the Barotse of Northern Rhodesia.* Manchester: Manchester University Press, for the Rhodes-Livingstone Institute, 1955.

GLUCKMAN, MAX. "Social Anthropology in Central Africa", *Human Problems in British Central Africa,* The Rhodes-Livingstone Journal, No. 20, 1956, pp. 1-27.

HOLLEMAN, J. F. *Shona Customary Law with Reference to Kinship, Marriage, the Family and the Estate.* Cape Town: Oxford University Press, for the Rhodes-Livingstone Institute, 1952.

HUGHES, A. J. B. *Kin, Caste and Nation Among the Rhodesian Ndebele.* Rhodes-Livingstone Papers No. 25, Manchester: Manchester University Press, 1956.

JASPAN, M. A. *The Ila-Tonga Peoples of North-Western Rhodesia.* Ethnographic Survey of Africa: West Central Africa, Part IV. London: The International African Institute, 1951.

KUPER, H.; HUGHES, A. J. B.; and VAN VELSEN, J. *The Shona and Ndebele of Southern Rhodesia.* Ethnographic Survey of Africa: Southern Africa, Part IV. London: The International African Institute, 1955.

MCCULLOCH, MERRAN. *The Southern Lunda and Related Peoples.* (Northern Rhodesia, Angola, Belgian Congo.) Ethnographic Survey of Africa: West Central Africa, Part I. London: The International African Institute, 1951.

MITCHELL, J. CLYDE. "The Political Organization of the Yao of Southern Nyasaland", *African Studies,* Vol. 8, No. 3, September 1949, pp. 141-59.

MITCHELL, J. C. "A Note on the Urbanization of Africans on the Copperbelt", *Human Problems in British Central Africa,* No. 12, 1951, pp. 20-7.

MITCHELL, J. CLYDE. "An Outline of the Social Structure of the Malemia Area", *Nyasaland Journal,* Vol. 4, No. 2, July 1951, pp. 15-48.

MITCHELL, J. CLYDE. *The Kalela Dance.* Manchester: Manchester University Press, for the Rhodes-Livingstone Institute (Papers No. 27), 1956.

MITCHELL, J. CLYDE. *The Yao Village:* a study in the social structure of a Nyasaland tribe. Manchester: Manchester University Press, for the Rhodes-Livingstone Institute, 1956.

READE, M. *The Ngoni of Nyasaland.* London: Oxford University Press, for the Rhodes-Livingstone Institute, 1956.

RICHARDS, A. I. *Land, Labour and Diet in Northern Rhodesia.* London: Oxford University Press, for the International Institute of African Languages and Cultures, 1939.

RICHARDS, AUDREY I. *Bemba Marriage and Present Economic Conditions.* Livingstone: Rhodes-Livingstone Institute, 1940.

TEW, MARY. *Peoples of the Lake Nyasa Region.* Ethnographic Survey of Africa: East Central Africa, Part I. London: Oxford University Press, for the International African Institute, 1950.

TURNER, V. W. *The Lozi Peoples of North Western Rhodesia.* Ethnographic Survey of Africa: West Central Africa, Part III. London: International African Institute, 1952.

TURNER, V. W. *Schism and Continuity in an African Society.* Manchester: Manchester University Press, for the Rhodes-Livingstone Institute, 1957.

WHITELEY, WILFRED, and others. I. *Bemba and Related Peoples of Northern Rhodesia . . . with a Contribution on the Ambo* by B. Stefaniszyn, S.J. II. *Peoples of the Lower Luapula Valley,* by J. Slaski. Ethnographic Survey of Africa: East Central Africa, Part II. London: The International African Institute, 1951.

WILSON, GODFREY B. *An Essay on the Economics of Detribalization in Northern Rhodesia.* Parts I and II. Livingstone: The Rhodes-Livingstone Institute (Publications Nos. 5 and 6), 1941-2.

WILSON, GODFREY, and MONICA. *The Analysis of Social Change.* Based on observations in Central Africa. Cambridge: The University Press, 1945 (2d printing 1954).

C. *Economics*

Board of Trade: The African Native Market in the Federation of Rhodesia and Nyasaland. Prepared by the United Kingdom Trade Commissioner, Salisbury. London: H.M.S.O., 1954.

DEANE, PHYLLIS. *Colonial Social Accounting.* Cambridge: The University Press, 1953. (National Institute of Economic and Social Research, Economic and Social Studies, No. XI.)

Development Plan, 1957-1961. Presented to the Federal Assembly, 27th June, 1957. Salisbury: Government Printer, 1957.

Investment in the Federation of Rhodesia and Nyasaland: Basic Information for United States Businessmen. Washington, D. C.: U. S. Department of Commerce, 1956.

Outline of Agrarian Problems and Policy in Nyasaland. Zomba: Government Printer, 1955.

Report of the Commission Appointed to Enquire into the Financial and Economic Position of Northern Rhodesia. (Sir Alan Pim and A. W. Milligan, Commissioners.) Col. 145. London: H.M.S.O., 1938.

Report of the Commission of Inquiry into the Future of European Farming. (L. G. Troup, Chairman.) Lusaka: Government Printer, 1954.

Report of the Commission of Inquiry into the Tenure of Agricultural Land. (L. G. Troup, Chairman.) Lusaka: Government Printer, 1954.

"Statistical Review of the Federation in 1954", *Monthly Digest of Statistics,* special supplementary issue, July 1955. Salisbury: Central African Statistical Office.

WOODRUFF, H. W. *Economic Conditions in the Federation of Rhodesia and Nyasaland.* Overseas Economic Surveys Series, London: H.M.S.O., 1955.

Newspapers

European:

Rhodesia Herald. Salisbury, daily.
Central African Post. Lusaka, daily.
Chronicle. Bulawayo, daily.
Nyasaland Times. Blantyre, daily.
The Citizen. Salisbury, weekly.

African:

African Daily News. Salisbury, daily.
Bantu Mirror. Salisbury, weekly.
African Weekly. Salisbury, weekly.
African Eagle. Salisbury, weekly.
Chapupu. Salisbury, bi-monthly.

Other Periodicals

Central African Examiner. Salisbury, fortnightly.
Concord. Salisbury, monthly.
Congress Circular. Lusaka.
East Africa and Rhodesia. London, weekly.
Federation of Rhodesia and Nyasaland Newsletter. London: Office of the High Commission for the Federation, weekly.
Human Problems in British Central Africa. Journal of the Rhodes-Livingstone Institute. Manchester University Press, bi-annual.
K.W.A.C.A. (Nyasaland African Congress.) Blantyre.
Monthly Digest of Statistics. Salisbury: Central African Statistical Office.

KENYA

The literature relating to the study of government and politics of Kenya, though seemingly extensive, is very uneven, and at times extremely partisan. As yet, there is no modern comprehensive study of political change of this multi-racial territory, though M. Dilley, *British Policy in Kenya Colony,* is a well documented study covering the period 1900 to 1935. D. H. Rawcliffe, *The Struggle for Kenya,* though not professing to be a scholarly treatment, is probably the best and most useful account of the immediate post-World War II years. Elspeth Huxley, *White Man's Country,* is a very readable and sympathetic study of white settlement and the life of Lord Delamere, Kenya's most famous settler. W. K. Hancock, in his *Survey of British Commonwealth Affairs,* Vol. I, has a brief but lucid analysis of the Indian question in the 1920's. Both W. McGregor Ross, *Kenya from Within,* and the works of Norman Leys written in the 1920's, are critical of white colonists and government policy. M. F. Hill, *The Dual Policy in Kenya,* is a collection of articles in book form written by the editor of one of Kenya's more important weekly newspapers. S. and K. Aaronovitch, *Crisis in Kenya,* written immediately after World War II, is an analysis of political and social development from a left-wing point of view. The student will find *Race and Politics in Kenya* by Elspeth Huxley and Margery Perham, a novel introduction to various problems in the form of a debate between the authors.

Many articles and books have been written about various aspects of the Mau Mau rebellion. L. S. B. Leakey, *Mau Mau and the Kikuyu* and *Defeating Mau Mau,* are considered the most authoritative account of its causes and organization. J. C. Carothers, in *The Psychology of Mau Mau,* provides another approach to an understanding of Mau Mau. Montagu Slater, *The Trial of Jomo Kenyatta,* is a detailed study of the trial of the man charged with organizing Mau Mau. It is, therefore, of particular value to read Kenyatta, *Facing Mount Kenya,* an anthropological study of the Kikuyu.

The pamphlets tend, naturally, to be even more controversial in nature; one of the most interesting is Tom Mboya's *The Kenya Question,* which presents the modern African viewpoint. Of a more scholarly nature are the writings of Mary Parker on municipal government, and particularly her article "Race Relations and Political Development in Kenya". George Bennett's article on political organizations show the historical development of such bodies. The complexity of Kenya's problems has also led to the publication of numerous official reports on British policy. Of particular interest in the inter-war years was the question of closer union of the East African territories. The report of the 1954 Parliamentary Delegation to Kenya, under the chairmanship of Sir Walter Elliot, deals with the handling of the Mau Mau emergency. The official statement of the "Lyttelton Constitution" is to be found in *Kenya: Proposals for a Reconstruction of the Government* (1954). The 1957 constitutional changes have so far only been outlined; the full statement was not available before publication.

Published anthropological material on Kenya, useful to the students of politics, is at present more limited than in the other British territories. Some important studies have been made by E. E. Evans-Pritchard, G. Wilson and A. Southall on the Luo, P. Mayer on the Gusii, H. A. Fosbrooke on the Masai, G. W. B. Huntingford on the Nilo-Hamites, and G. Wagner on the Kavirondo Bantu. The works of L. S. B. Leakey and Jomo Kenyatta on the Kikuyu have already been mentioned; H. E. Lambert's study also contains valuable information. Arthur Phillips, *Report on Native Tribunals,* is of particular interest for this aspect of African political life.

Most of the information on the economic situation in Kenya comes from official reports. Land has always been the major question in Kenya; its occupation and use, from both the economic and political aspects, is the subject of many works. The *Report of the East Africa Royal Commission 1953-1955,* on land and population provides a thorough study of these problems, and its recommendations have important political implications. Summaries of this detailed document have been listed. Questions of labor, trade and communications have also been significant in Kenya; the most useful general survey of economic conditions is the Economist Intelligence Unit Report, *The Economy of East Africa: A Study of Trends.*

A. *Government and Politics*

1. *Official Publications*

a. *Great Britain*

Indians in Kenya: A Memorandum. Cmd. 1922. London: H.M.S.O., 1923.

Report of the East Africa Commission 1924. Cmd. 2387. London: H.M.S.O., 1925.

Tours in the Native Reserves and Native Development in Kenya. Cmd. 2537. London: H.M.S.O., 1926.

Future Policy in Regard to Eastern Africa. Cmd. 2904. London: H.M.S.O., 1927.

Report of Sir Samuel Wilson on his Visit to East Africa. Cmd. 3378. London: H.M.S.O., 1929.

Report of the Commission on Closer Union for the Dependencies in East and Central Africa. (Sir E. Hilton Young, Chairman.) Cmd. 3234. London: H.M.S.O., 1929.

Memorandum on Native Policy in East Africa. Cmd. 3573. London: H.M.S.O., 1930.

Report of the Joint Select Committee on Closer Union in East Africa. 3 Vols. H. C. Paper No. 156. London: H.M.S.O., 1931.

Statement of the Conclusion of His Majesty's Government in the United Kingdom as regards Closer Union in East Africa. Cmd. 3574. London: H.M.S.O., 1930.

Papers Relating to the Question of Closer Union of Kenya, Uganda and Tanganyika Territory. Col. 57. London: H.M.S.O., 1931.

Correspondence Arising from the Report of the Joint Select Committee on Closer Union in East Africa, 1931-32. Cmd. 4141. London: H.M.S.O., 1932.

Report of the Commission of Inquiry into the Administration of Justice in Kenya, Uganda and the Tanganyika Territory in Criminal Matters, May 1933, and Correspondence arising out of the Report. Col. 96. London: H.M.S.O., 1934.

Report of the Kenya Land Commission. (Sir Morris Carter, Chairman.) Cmd. 4556. London: H.M.S.O., 1934. *Evidence and Memoranda,* 3 vols. Col. 91. London: H.M.S.O., 1934.

Report of the Commission on Higher Education in East Africa. Col. 142. London: H.M.S.O., 1937.

Inter-territorial Organization in East Africa. Col. 191. London: H.M.S.O., 1945.

Inter-territorial Organization in East Africa: Revised Proposals. Col. 210. London: H.M.S.O., 1947.

The East Africa (High Commission) Order in Council 1947. Statutory Instruments No. 2863, 1947.

The East Africa (High Commission) (amendment) Order in Council, 1951. Statutory Instruments No. 2126, 1951.

Land and Population in East Africa: Exchange of correspondence between the Secretary of State for the Colonies and the Government of Kenya on the appointment of the Royal Commission. Col. 290. London: H.M.S.O., 1952.

Report to the Secretary of State for the Colonies by the Parliamentary Delegation to Kenya, January 1954. (Walter Elliot, Chairman.) Cmd. 9081. London: H.M.S.O., 1954.

Kenya: Proposals for a Reconstruction of the Government. Cmd. 9103. London: H.M.S.O., 1954.

Report of the East Africa Royal Commission 1953-1955. (Sir Hugh Dow, Chairman.) Cmd. 9475. London: H.M.S.O., 1955.

Despatches from the Governors of Kenya, Uganda and Tanganyika and from the Administrator, East Africa High Commission, commenting on the East Africa Royal Commission 1953-55 Report. Cmd. 9801. London: H.M.S.O., 1956.

b. Kenya

Report of the Local Government Commission. London: Crown Agents, for the Government of Kenya, 1927.

The Crown Lands (Amendment) Ordinance, 1938.

The Native Lands Trust Ordinance, 1938.

Land Control Ordinance, No. 22, 1944.

Proposals for the Reorganization of the Administration of Kenya. Sessional Paper No. 3. Nairobi: Government Printer, 1945.

Land Utilization and Settlement: A Statement of Government Policy. Nairobi: Government Printer, 1945.

PHILLIPS, ARTHUR. *Report of Native Tribunals.* Nairobi: Government Printer, 1945.

African Education: A Statement of Policy. Nairobi: Government Printer, 1951.

CAROTHERS, J. C. *The Psychology of Mau Mau.* Nairobi: Government Printer, 1954.

Legislative Council: Standing Orders and Letters Patent, Royal Instructions and Ordinances under which the Council functions. Brought together by A. W. Purvis, Clerk of the Legislative Council. Nairobi: Government Printer, 1954.

Report of the Commission on the Civil Services of the East African Territories and the East Africa High Commission 1953-54. (Sir David Lidbury, Chairman.) Report to the Chairman, East Africa High Commission, the Governors of Kenya, Uganda and Tanganyika, and the British Resident, Zanzibar. Government Printing Offices, Nairobi, Dar es Salaam, Entebbe and Zanzibar, and the Crown Agents for Oversea Governments. 1954.

Report of the Commissioner Appointed to Enquire into Methods for the Selection of African Representatives to the Legislative Council. (W. F. Coutts, Commissioner.) Nairobi: Government Printer, 1955.

Report of the Commissioner Appointed to Enquire into Methods for the Selection of African Representatives to the Legislative Council. (Statement of Government Policy.) Sessional Paper, No. 39. Nairobi: Government Printer, 1956.

2. *Unofficial Publications*

a. Books

AARONOVITCH, S. and K. *Crisis in Kenya.* London: Lawrence and Wishart, 1947.

ALTRINCHAM, LORD. *Kenya's Opportunity: Memories, Hopes and Ideas.* London: Faber and Faber, 1955.

BLIXEN, KAREN. *Out of Africa.* London: Penguin Books, 1954. (First published, 1937.)

BROCKWAY, FENNER. *African Journeys.* London: Gollancz, 1955.

COUPLAND, R. *East Africa and its Invaders:* from the earliest times to the death of Seyyid Said in 1856. Oxford: Clarendon Press, 1938.

COUPLAND, R. *The Exploitation of East Africa, 1856-1890:* the slave trade and the scramble. London: Faber and Faber, 1939.

CRANWORTH, LORD. *Kenya Chronicles.* London: Macmillan, 1939.

DILLEY, MARJORIE R. *British Policy in Kenya Colony.* New York: Nelson, 1937.

DRIBERG, J. H. *The East African Problem.* London: Williams and Norgate, 1930.

ELIOT, SIR CHARLES. *The East Africa Protectorate.* London: Edward Arnold, 1905.

EVANS, PETER. *Law and Disorder.* London: Secker and Warburg, 1956.

FARSON, NEGLEY. *Behind God's Back.* London: Gollancz, 1940.

FARSON, NEGLEY. *Last Chance in Africa.* London: Gollancz, 1951.

HARRIES, LYNDON P. *Islam in East Africa.* London: Parrett and Neves, 1954.

HATCH, JOHN. *New From Africa.* London: Dennis Dobson, 1956.

HILL, M. F. *The Dual Policy in Kenya.* Nakuru: Kenya Weekly News, 1944.

HILL, M. F. *Permanent Way: The Story of the Kenya and Uganda Railway.* Nairobi: East African Railways and Harbours, 1950.

HOBLEY, CHARLES W. *Kenya from Chartered Company to Crown Colony.* London: Witherby, 1929.

HUXLEY, ELSPETH. *White Man's Country: Lord Delamere and the Making of Kenya.* 2 Vols. London: Macmillan, 1935.

HUXLEY, ELSPETH, and PERHAM, MARGERY. *Race and Politics in Kenya.* London: Faber and Faber, revised edition, 1955.

LEAKEY, L. S. B. *Mau Mau and the Kikuyu.* London: Methuen, 1952.

LEAKEY, L. S. B. *Defeating Mau Mau.* London: Methuen, 1954.
LEYS, NORMAN M. *Kenya.* London: Hogarth Press, 1924.
LEYS, NORMAN M. *A Last Chance in Kenya.* London: Hogarth Press, 1931.
LEYS, NORMAN M. *The Colour Bar in East Africa.* London: Hogarth Press, 1940.
LIPSCOMB, J. F. *White Africans.* London: Faber and Faber, 1955.
LIPSCOMB, J. F. *We Built a Country.* London: Faber and Faber, 1956.
MITCHELL, PHILIP E. *African Afterthoughts.* London: Hutchinson, 1954.
MOCKERIE, PARMENAS GITHENDU. *An African Speaks for his People.* London, 1934.
OLIVER, ROLAND. *The Missionary Factor in East Africa.* London: Longmans, Green, 1952.
PANKHURST, RICHARD. *Kenya: The History of Two Nations.* London: Independent Publishing Company, 1955.
RAWCLIFFE, D. H. *The Struggle for Kenya.* London: Gollancz, 1954.
ROSS, W. MCGREGOR. *Kenya from Within: A Short Political History.* London: Allen and Unwin, 1927.
SALVADORI, MAX. *La Colonisation Européenne au Kenya.* Paris: Larose Editeurs, 1938.
SLATER, MONTAGU. *The Trial of Jomo Kenyatta.* London: Secker and Warburg, 1955.
THURNWALD, RICHARD C. *Black and White in East Africa.* London: Routledge, 1935.
WILLS, COLIN. *Who Killed Kenya?* London: Dennis Dobson, 1953.
WILSON, CHRISTOPHER. *Kenya's Warning.* Nairobi: English Press, 1954.

b. Articles and pamphlets

AFRICA BUREAU. *Future of East Africa.* A summary of the report of the Royal Commission with an index to the report. London, 1955.
AFRICA BUREAU. *Reflections on the Report of the Royal Commission on East Africa.* London, 1955.
BENNETT, GEORGE. "The Development of Political Organizations in Kenya", *Political Studies,* Vol. 5, No. 2, June 1957, pp. 113-30.
THE BRITISH SURVEY. *Kenya: Mau Mau and the Kikuyu Problem.* London: British Society for International Understanding, May 1954.
BROCKWAY, FENNER. *Why Mau Mau? An Analysis and a Remedy.* London: Congress of Peoples against Imperialism, March 1953.
CAVENDISH-BENTINCK, F. *Indians and the Kenya Highlands.* Nairobi: The East African Standard, 1939.
EAST AFRICAN INSTITUTE OF SOCIAL RESEARCH: June Conference, 1952. *The Present Position of the Lower Chiefs.* Including: K. Cowley, "The Native Authority System in Kenya", and G. Harris, "The Position of Lower Chiefs in Taita". Bound mimeograph.
EVANS, M. N. "Local Government in the African Areas of Kenya", *Journal of African Administration,* Vol. 7, No. 3, July 1955, pp. 123-7.
FABIAN COLONIAL BUREAU. *Kenya, White Man's Country?* Research Series, No. 7. London, 1944.
FABIAN COLONIAL BUREAU. *Kenya Controversy.* Controversy Series, No. 4, London, 1947.

FABIAN COLONIAL BUREAU. *East African Future.* Controversy Series, No. 9. London, 1952.

FABIAN COLONIAL BUREAU. *Opportunity in Kenya.* Research Series, No. 162. London, 1953.

FRANCIS, E. CAREY. "Kenya's Problems as Seen by a Schoolmaster in Kikuyu Country", *African Affairs,* Vol. 54, No. 216, July 1955, pp. 186-95.

GRIGG, SIR EDWARD (LORD ALTRINCHAM). *The Constitutional Problem in Kenya.* Cust Foundation Lecture 1933. University College, Nottingham.

KILSON, MARTIN L. "Land and the Kikuyu: A Study of the Relationship between Land and Kikuyu Political Movements", *Journal of Negro History,* Vol. 40, No. 2, April 1955, pp. 103-53.

Kenya: Report of the Parliamentary Delegation, January-February 1957. (Sir Thomas Dugdale, Leader.) London: Commonwealth Parliamentary Association, 1957.

KNOWLES, E. J. F. "Foundations of Government in Kenya", *Journal of African Administration,* Vol. 6, No. 3, July 1954, pp. 137-9.

LA FONTAINE, S. H., and MOWER, J. H. *Local Government in Kenya: Its Origins and Development.* Nairobi: Eagle Press, 1955.

MASON, PHILIP. *A New Deal in East Africa.* London: Royal Institute of International Affairs, 1955.

The Native Lands Trust Ordinance, 1938.

MASON, PHILIP. "The Plural Society of Kenya", INCIDI (International Institute of Differing Civilizations), *Ethnic and Cultural Pluralism in Intertropical Communities.* Report of the 30th Meeting held in Lisbon, April 1957, pp. 325-37. Brussels, 1957.

MONKHOUSE, PATRICK. "The Mau Mau in Kenya", *Manchester Guardian,* 12, 17, 18, 20, 24 November, 1952.

NOON, JOHN A. "Political Developments in East Africa", in Calvin W. Stillman ed. *Africa and the Modern World,* Chicago: University of Chicago Press, 1955.

PARKER, MARY. *Political and Social Aspects of the Development of Municipal Government in Kenya with Special Reference to Nairobi.* London: Colonial Office, n.d. (1949?) (mimeograph).

PARKER, MARY. "Municipal Government and the Growth of African Political Institutions in the Urban Areas of Kenya", *Zaïre,* Vol. 3, June 1949, pp. 649-62.

PARKER, MARY. "Race Relations and Political Development in Kenya", *African Affairs,* Vol. 50, No. 198, January 1951, pp. 41-52.

PARKER, MARY. *How Kenya is Governed.* Nairobi: Eagle Press, revised edition, 1955.

ROSENTIEL, ANNETTE. "An Anthropological Approach to the Mau Mau Problem", *Political Science Quarterly,* Vol. 68, No. 3, September 1953, pp. 419-32.

SCOTT, H. S. "European Settlement and Native Development in Kenya", *African Affairs,* Vol. 35, No. 139, April 1936, pp. 178-90.

VASEY, E. A. "Economic and Political Trends in Kenya", *African Affairs,* Vol. 55, No. 219, April 1956, pp. 101-8.

WHITELEY, W. H. "The Changing Position of Swahili in East Africa", *Africa,* Vol. 26, No. 4, October 1956, pp. 343-53.

c. Political pamphlets

African Unofficial Members Organisation. *Method of Electing African Members of Kenya Legislative Council.* Nairobi, 1955.

Electors' Union. *An Outline of Policy for the Colony and Protectorate of Kenya.* Nairobi, 1946.

Electors' Union. *Kenya Plan.* Nairobi, 1949.

Electors' Union. *The Kenya Land Problem: A History of African and European Land Settlement.* Nairobi, 1952.

Electors' Union. *Report of the Conference Standing Committee* set up by the delegates who attended the "Truce" Conference on October 4th, 1954. Nairobi, 1955.

Kenya Indian Congress. *Statement of Policy.* Nairobi, 12 March 1955.

Kenya Indian Congress. *The Presidential Address* by N. S. Mangat, at the Twenty-fourth Session at Nakuru, August 1956. Nairobi, 1956.

Koinange, Mbiyu. *The People of Kenya Speak for Themselves.* Detroit: Kenya Publication Fund, 1955.

Mboya, Tom. *The Kenya Question: An African Answer.* London: Fabian Colonial Bureau, 1956.

B. Anthropology

Butt, Audrey. *The Nilotes of the Anglo-Egyptian Sudan and Uganda.* Ethnographic Survey of Africa: East Central Africa, Part IV. London: The International African Institute, 1952.

Cagnola, Father C. *The Akikuyu.* Nyeri: The Mission Printing School, 1933.

Evans-Pritchard, E. E. "Luo Tribes and Clans", *Human Problems in British Central Africa,* the Rhodes-Livingstone Journal, No. 7, 1949, pp. 24-40.

Fosbrooke, H. A. "An Administrative Survey of the Masai Social System", *Tanganyika Notes,* Vol. 26, 1948, pp. 1-50.

Gulliver, P. H. *The Family Herds: A Study of Two Pastoral Tribes in East Africa, The Jie and Turkana.* London: Routledge and Kegan Paul, 1955.

Hobley, C. W. *Bantu Beliefs and Magic:* with particular reference to the Kikuyu and Kamba tribes of Kenya Colony. London: Witherby, 1938. (First published, 1922.)

Huntingford, G. W. B. *The Nandi of Kenya:* Tribal control in a pastoral society. London: Routledge and Kegan Paul, 1953.

Huntingford, G. W. B. *The Southern Nilo-Hamites.* Ethnographic Survey of Africa: East Central Africa, Part VIII. London: The International African Institute, 1953.

Huntingford, G. W. B., and Bell, C. R. V. *East African Background.* London: Longmans, Green, second edition, 1950.

Huxley, Elspeth. *Red Strangers.* London: Chatto and Windus, 1939. (An anthropological novel.)

Kenyatta, Jomo. *Facing Mount Kenya.* London: Secker and Warburg, 1938.

Lambert, H. E. *Kikuyu Social and Political Institutions.* London: Oxford University Press, for the International African Institute, 1956.

Mayer, Philip. *The Lineage Principle in Gusii Society.* Memorandum No. 24. London: Oxford University Press, for the International African Institute, 1949.

MIDDLETON, JOHN. *The Kikuyu and Kamba of Kenya.* Ethnographic Survey of Africa: East Central Africa, Part V. London: The International African Institute, 1953.

PERISTIANY, J. G. *The Social Institutions of the Kipsigis.* London: Routledge, 1939.

PRINS, A. H. J. *The Coastal Tribes of the North-Eastern Bantu* (Pokomo, Nyika, Teita.) Ethnographic Survey of Africa: East Central Africa, Part III. London: The International African Institute, 1952.

PRINS, A. H. J. *East African Age-Class Systems.* Djakarta: J. B. Wolters, 1953.

SOUTHALL, A. *Lineage Formation Among the Luo.* International African Institute, Memorandum No. 26. London: Oxford University Press, 1952.

WAGNER, GUNTHER. *The Bantu of the North Kavirondo.* London: Oxford University Press, for the International African Institute, Vol. I, 1949; Vol. II, 1956.

WAGNER, GUNTHER. "The Political Organization of the Bantu of Kavirondo", in M. Fortes and E. E. Evans-Pritchard, *ed. African Political Systems.* London: Oxford University Press, for the International African Institute, 1950.

C. Economics

Certain Questions in Kenya: Report by the Financial Commissioner (Lord Moyne). Cmd. 4093. London: H.M.S.O., 1932.

Report of the Commission Appointed to Enquire into and Report on the Financial Position and System of Taxation in Kenya. (Sir Alan Pim, Commissioner.) Col. 116. London: H.M.S.O., 1936.

HUMPHREY, N., LAMBERT, H. E., and WYN HARRIS, P. *The Kikuyu Lands.* Nairobi: Government Printer, 1945.

Labour Conditions in East Africa. Report by Major G. St. J. Orde Browne. Col. 193. London: H.M.S.O., 1946.

BASSETT, R. H. *Report and Recommendations on the Development of Agricultural Marketing in Kenya.* Nairobi: Government Printer, 1946.

HUMPHREY, NORMAN. *The Liguru and the Land.* Nairobi: Government Printer, 1947.

NORTHCOTT, C. H., *ed. African Labour Efficiency Survey, 1947.* Colonial Research Publication No. 3. London: H.M.S.O., 1947.

MITCHELL, SIR PHILIP. *The Agrarian Problem in Kenya.* Nairobi: Government Printer, 1947.

MATHESON, J. K., and BOVILL, E. W. *East African Agriculture.* London: Oxford University Press, 1950.

VASEY, E. A. *Report on African Housing in Townships and Trading Centres.* Nairobi: Government Printer, 1950.

African Development in Kenya, 1946-1955: Land, Livestock and Water. Progress report issued by the Member for Agriculture and Natural Resources, November, 1952. Nairobi: Government Printer, 1953.

Report of an Inquiry into the General Economy of Farming in the Highlands . . . (L. G. Troup, Commissioner.) Nairobi: Government Printer, 1953.

Report of the Committee on African Wages. (F. W. Carpenter, Chairman.) Parts 1-3. Nairobi: Government Printer, 1954.

A Plan to Intensify the Development of African Agriculture in Kenya. Compiled by R. J. M. Swynnerton. Nairobi: Government Printer, 1955.

Progress Report on the Three-and-a-half-year Development Plan. Sessional Paper No. 97. Nairobi: Government Printer, 1955.

The Economy of East Africa: A Study of Trends. Prepared by the Economist Intelligence Unit, for the East African Railways and Harbours Administration. Nairobi, 1955.

LEAKEY, L. S. B. "The Economics of Kikuyu Tribal Life", *East African Economics Review,* Vol. 3, No. 1, July 1956, pp. 165-80.

Statistical Abstract 1955. Nairobi: Government Printer, 1957.

Newspapers

European:

East African Standard. Nairobi, daily.
Mombasa Times. Mombasa, daily.
Sunday Post, Nairobi, weekly.
Kenya Weekly News. Nakuru, weekly.

Asian:

The Goan Voice. Nairobi, weekly.
Colonial Times. Nairobi, weekly.
The Citizen. Nairobi, weekly.

African:

Baraza. Nairobi, daily.
Nyanza Times. Kisumu, weekly.

Other Periodicals

Comment. Nairobi, weekly.

East Africa and Rhodesia. London, weekly.

East African Statistical Department: *Quarterly Economic and Statistical Bulletin.* Nairobi: East Africa High Commission.

The East African Economics Review. Journal of the Economics Club of Kenya and the Uganda Economics Society. Nairobi, bi-annual.

Kenya Calling: Weekly News Digest. Nairobi: Department of Information.

Kenya Today. Nairobi: Department of Information, quarterly.

The Voice of Kenya. London, irregularly published, 1953-1955.

Index